The Literacy Kit

Persuade and Analyse

Geoff Barton

OXFORD
UNIVERSITY PRESS
Great Clarendon Street, Oxford OX2 6DP

Oxford University Press is a department of the University of Oxford.

It furthers the University's objective of excellence in research, scholarship, and education by publishing worldwide in

Oxford New York

Auckland Bangkok Buenos Aires Cape Town Chennai
Dar es Salaam Delhi Hong Kong Istanbul Karachi Kolkata
Kuala Lumpur Madrid Melbourne Mexico City Mumbai Nairobi
São Paulo Shanghai Singapore Taipei Tokyo Toronto

with an associated company in Berlin

Oxford is a registered trade mark of Oxford University Press
in the UK and in certain other countries

© Geoff Barton 2001

First published 2001

The moral rights of the authors have been asserted

Database right Oxford University Press (maker)

ACKNOWLEDGEMENTS

Crown Copyright material, extracts from 'Sun Safety' article from wiredforheatlh.gov.uk website (DH and DfEE) and from 'Sun Know How' article from doh.gov.uk website (DH), are reproduced under Class Licence Number C01P0000148 with the permission of the Controller of HMSO and the Queen's Printer for Scotland.

We are also grateful to the following for permission to reprint copyright material:

Abbot Mead Vickers BBDO and the RSPCA for script of 'Swim' radio advertisement

The Bristol Group Ltd for advertisement for the 'Barlow Knee Support'

Cathedral Dental Practice for leaflet issued by practice

English and Media Centre for review by Sam Flintham-Ward first published in *English & Media Magazine*, No 42/3, November 2000

Friends of the Earth for extract from www.foe.co.uk website

R & W Heap (Publishing) Co Ltd for advertisement 'A Startling Memory Feat That You Can Do', copyright © R & W Heap (Publishing) Co Ltd

Howstuffworks Inc for extracts from 'How rainforests work' by Tom Harris from www.howstuffworks.com website

The Independent for 'Let's Get Physical' by Louise Osmond and Phil Cool, *The Indy*, 5.10.89, extract from 'The complete guide to British Theme Parks' by Martyn Symington, *The Independent*, 25.3.00, and extracts from '50 Best ... White knuckle rides' by Emma Haughton, from www.independent.co.uk/travel website

Ivillage Inc for extracts from 'Four More Excuses to Eat Chocolate' by Sue Gilbert from www.ivillage.com website

The Estate of James MacGibbon for Stevie Smith: 'Not Waving but Drowning'

from *Collected Poems of Stevie Smith* (Penguin Modern Classics), copyright © 1972 Stevie Smith

The Random House Group Ltd for 'A Recollection' by Frances Cornford from *Collected Poems* (Cresset Press)

Save the Children for 'Take Children Seriously' advertisement

The Star for opinion article: 'It's sweets and sour' from *The Star*, 15.7.93

Times Educational Supplement for 'It's For You' by Cassandra Hilland, *TES*, 5.5.00, copyright © Times Supplements Ltd 2000; and 'Rules too tight for comfort' by Katharine Frazer-Barnes, *TES*, 5.11.99, copyright © Times Supplements Ltd 1999

A P Watt Ltd on behalf of the author for review by India Knight: 'Harry is Too Horrible' first published in *The Sunday Times*, 16 July 2000

and to Tom Fullam, student at Thurston Community College, for use of his work.

We have tried to trace and contact all copyright holders before publication. If notified the publishers will be pleased to rectify any errors or omissions at the earliest opportunity.

We are grateful to the following for permission to reproduce photographs:

Photodisc/Mark Mason studios (cover); Peter Adams/Ace, p77; Jane Alexander/Photofusion, p3; Julia Bayne/Robert Harding Picture Library, p103; Paul Baldesare/Photofusion p115; John Birdsall pp 54, 92, 121; Cheryl A. Ertelt/RSPCA, p101; Eye Ubiquitous pp 20, 41; Stephen Frailey/Photonica p57; Andrew Forsyth/RSPCA p99; Robert Harding Picture Library pp 67, 81, 112; Nancy Honey/Photonica p6; G Montgomery/Photofusion p107; Photographer's Library pp 29, 84, 105, 108; Photonica p25; Powerstock p78; Estate of Janet Stone p133; Christa Stadtler/Photofusion p27; SuperStock pp 37, 125; Topham Picturepoint pp 17, 46, 72; Christopher Wadsworth/Photonica p129; John Walmsley p52; Universal Pictorial Press p132; Zefa-Madison/Powerstock p13; Cromwell Productions p95; Stockbye pp 22, 69, 71; Digital Vision pp 51, 55, 63, 110, 114; Photodisc pp 74, 126; Corel pp 100, 104, 123, 124, 130, 131

Other photographs by Rebecca Crabtree

The cartoon illustrations are by David Semple.

A CIP catalogue record for this book is available from the British Library.

ISBN 0 19 832037 X

10 9 8 7 6 5 4 3 2

Printed in Spain by Graficas Estella SA.

Orders and enquiries to Customer Services:

Tel: 01536 741068 **Fax:** 01536 454519

Contents

Introduction

Persuade and Analyse is a central part of *The Literacy Kit*. It provides the core texts you will need for developing pupils' reading, writing and spoken work.

You may have used one of the starter activities in the **Lesson Starters** boxes to kick the lesson off, and **OHTs** from the relevant pack to initiate whole-class discussion of text types. Now comes the developmental stage, in which students focus on the specific word-, sentence- and text-level objectives of the *Framework for Teaching English 11–14*.

This Students' Book provides you with texts that are closely mapped to all the objectives and organized on a year-by-year basis, enabling you to plan more carefully and to ensure that essential text types are covered in each year. The **Objectives** box at the head of each text extract details the objectives addressed.

The texts always begin with an **Introduction**. This is a brisk, context-setting starter which tunes pupils into the type of text they are looking at. It will get them focusing on the language features and issues they can expect to be dealing with. You may want to develop this, asking pupils to make predictions before they start to read the text.

The **texts** themselves have been carefully selected to highlight some key features of structure and language, and to match the appropriate levels of interest and ability of pupils in different year groups. You'll find plenty of texts on contemporary subjects that should appeal to boys and girls aged 11–14.

The questions which follow provide for two levels of response. **Understanding the text** asks straightforward, fact-spotting questions. Don't underestimate the importance of these: they are the questions that quickly build pupils' confidence in skimming and scanning, helping them to identify key points quickly.

Interpreting the text offers more open-ended questions. Here pupils will need to give more reflective responses, often writing short paragraphs explaining and justifying their thoughts.

The **Language and structure** section highlights the new emphasis on language skills within the Framework. These are not arid, 'spot the split infinitive' style questions. Their focus is on language in use, getting pupils looking at writers' language decisions, cataloguing features of the text and then commenting on effect. This is the central part of the literacy process – emphasizing effect, and not simply spotting language features.

The **Writing activity** focuses on an aspect of the text and gets pupils responding in writing in a more developed way. They may be asked to practise a language skill in greater detail, or to rewrite part of the text in a different style. Importantly, this is the part of the process that shifts the emphasis from reading to writing. Having explored features of the writer's approach in a text, pupils now begin to write for themselves. It is part of the process of scaffolding writing.

Each unit concludes with an **Extended writing** task. Here the emphasis on developing pupils' writing skills is consolidated. These are bigger, more ambitious tasks which link back to the texts that pupils have been exploring. The tasks are scaffolded with suggestions, hints and, often, starter sentences. This approach should help pupils in the transition from dependent to independent writers.

Speaking and listening is integral to all English work and we know that you will be talking to students about their perceptions of texts throughout the process. We have also built in specific speaking and listening tasks where they develop language skills, or provide an opportunity to meet one of the *Framework* objectives.

In the **Teacher's Book** you will find a wealth of related resources, and the **OHT** pack provides those all-important acetates for a shared, whole-class focus on texts.

The Literacy Kit is, as you can see, a completely integrated scheme. I've been using it with my students here in Suffolk and the response to the variety, the rapid pace, and the sheer range of materials has been terrific – even from my more reluctant pupils!

I hope it proves similarly enjoyable and useful for you, helping you with the planning and delivery of the *Framework* in a lively and systematic way. Most of all, I hope your students have fun with the huge variety of new resources here.

Your feedback, via the website, would be very welcome.

Geoff Barton
www.oup.com/uk/litkit

v

What is persuasive writing?

Purpose and audience

Persuasive writing may express a point of view, or aim to change your opinions, or try to get you to buy something. It might be a letter or essay, an advertisement, a leaflet, or a television programme. Writers will often draw you into their world so that you can see things from their point of view. They will work on your feelings to try to get you to agree with them.

Text level features

The text may use **illustrations** to help persuade you – for example, in an advertisement a picture of a country scene may aim to suggest that a product is natural. It may use different **layout features** – such as font sizes – to make an impact. The writing may start with an **opening statement**, setting out the writer's views, and then go through them in more detail. The text will emphasize **key points**, and there will be **logical links** to guide the reader through the argument. The writer may use **humour** to get the reader on her or his side.

Sentence level features

The writer may use the **first person** (I and me) to express opinions, or may write using the **third person** (she, he, they) to create a more impersonal effect. Advertising will often be much more direct in its tone, using the **second person** and **imperatives** (commands): 'Phone us now for your free starter-pack'. Persuasive writing will usually be **active**, with short sentences for effect ('Don't you believe it!'). It will often use the **present tense**.

Word level features

Writers will choose powerful words to influence the reader, so you might expect **emotive** words like *clash, fury, fiasco, disaster*, with writers sometimes overstating ideas (using **exaggerated language**) to make their point. In advertising, writers may use **word play** for effect, such as 'Beanz Meanz Heinz'.

Getting your point across
Rules Too Tight for Comfort

OBJECTIVES

This text puts forward a strongly argued point of view. These are the objectives you will be studying:

- Word level: *connectives*
- Sentence level: *tense management*, *active and passive*, *starting paragraphs*, *main point of paragraph*, and *sequencing paragraphs*
- Reading: *note-making*, *identify main ideas*, *infer and deduce*, *non-fiction style* (how writers match language and organization to their intentions), *language choices*, and *endings*
- Writing: *drafting process*, *organize texts appropriately*, *develop logic*, *express a view*, and *validate an argument* (find ways to back it up)

Introduction

This text is about having to wear school uniform. It was written by a 15-year-old student who expresses her opinions and tries to persuade us to agree with them. The article appeared in the *Times Educational Supplement*, a newspaper aimed at teachers. When you have studied this persuasive text, you can try writing one of your own.

Rules Too Tight for Comfort

Uniforms have a point but it's taken too far, says pupil Katharine Frazer-Barnes

THE IDEA OF SCHOOL UNIFORMS is to help create an atmosphere of equality between workmates. But are some schools getting carried away with what pupils can and can't wear?

When I moved up to secondary school, I was thrilled at the prospect of wearing a bright yellow shirt and a blazer which had the consistency of cardboard. I couldn't understand why some of the older students were so determined not to wear them; I was young, I was awe-struck, I was 11-years-old.

So here I am, in Year 11, with my GCSEs looming, and I've turned into one of those typical 15-year-olds whom I couldn't understand when I started here.

Just the other day I was chastised for the 'amount of metal' I was wearing on my fingers, and a couple of weeks back a friend, who had dyed the tips of her hair red, was told to remove the colour or she'd get into trouble. I thought her hair looked wicked, but I wasn't going to argue with the head of year.

Back in my young, awe-struck days, I was under the impression that school uniform consisted of clothes alone: now I find that it dictates how many earrings you can wear, what colour your hair is, what footwear you can wear – even how your shirts should be worn.

Uniform has created many a fun game for us older students; one of the most popular is 'try to get into assembly without getting pulled over for incorrect uniform'. The idea is to avoid the watchful gaze of the prefects and staff while maintaining a sense of individual style. Some of us manage to pull it off, others end up in trouble. I have managed to avoid trouble so far.

I can see the point of uniform – in the clothes sense at least. Health and safety issues hold great importance in any school. A student who is working a fretsaw with massive clumps of metal hanging from her ears is a danger to herself.

And as staff keep telling us, it stops any feelings of inadequacy if you're not wearing the right clothes. But this is not a strong enough argument for making uniform compulsory; after all, there are so many ways to wear uniform, who says that you won't get ridiculed for the way you wear it?

Uniform is basically common sense. There is a place for it: if you're working machinery you don't want things to get caught. And if you're studying food technology, a grubby leather jacket is not hygienic.

But why are there rules on, for example, hair colour? As far as I know, (although the scientists may want to put me straight) dyeing your hair has absolutely no effect on your brain power.

And then there's uniform-induced bullying.

My younger school days were filled with fear at the prospect of an encounter with any of the pupils from neighbouring schools who when they saw anyone in a yellow shirt used to intimidate and in some, sadly not so rare, cases cause them harm. I was once pushed into the road by such bullies and for months afterwards hid inside a big pink duffel coat.

I suppose the experience and various incidents that have happened to friends have made me think quite hard about uniform. Consequently I've been strongly 'anti' since the middle of Year 8. Uniform has caused me far more problems than I thought any sort of code ever would. And in addition, whatever happened to freedom of expression?

And, if you want to talk to me about this article, I'll be the one with the orange hair, bejewelled fingers and unlaced Doc Martens. See you in detention.

UNDERSTANDING THE TEXT

1 What was the writer's attitude to uniform when she moved to secondary school?

2 How has her attitude changed now that she is in Year 11?

3 When did her attitude to uniform become strongly 'anti'?

4 What was the experience that helped change her opinion?

5 What has she been in trouble at school for wearing?

6 What game do she and her friends play with their uniforms?

INTERPRETING THE TEXT

7 The text gives us a good idea of what the writer and her school are like.

  a What impression do you get of the writer? What sort of person is she? Support your answer with examples.

  b What impression do you get of the school she attends? Choose the word from those below that best describes it, and write a sentence to explain your choice:

    strict   fun   old-fashioned   formal   informal   traditional

8 Re-read the article, making notes of its key points about school uniform. Based on your notes, make a list of the arguments for and against enforcing uniform rules.

LANGUAGE AND STRUCTURE

1 A well-structured text will use a different paragraph for each new idea. Look at the first five paragraphs of the article. Use the table to match up each paragraph with its topic.

Paragraph number (1-5)	Topic
	Looks back to when the writer was younger
	Gives an example of how she got into trouble
	Introduces the issue and raises a question about it
	Adds detail to what uniform actually means
	Describes how her attitude has now changed

2 a Now do the same for paragraphs 6, 7 and 8 – define what they are about.

b Does the writer's organization of her paragraphs help to get her arguments across? Say why or why not.

3 Persuasive texts often use the present tense. Look again at paragraphs 1 and 2. What tense is each paragraph written in? What is the reason for this?

4 Look at the way the writer signals that paragraph 2 is moving to a different period of her life: 'When I moved up …' This uses the past tense ('moved') and the discourse marker 'when'.

a Which words link paragraph 3 back to paragraph 2?

b Which words link paragraph 4 back to paragraph 3?

5 Most persuasive texts use the active voice to express ideas rather than the passive. Look at how one sentence from this text would be different in the passive voice:

Active	Passive
Uniform has created many a fun game for us older students …	Many a fun game has been created for us older students by uniform

Why do you think it suits the writer to use the active voice throughout?

6 Like many writers of persuasive texts, Katharine Frazer-Barnes uses humour, including exaggerations such as these:

… *a blazer which had the* **consistency** *of* **cardboard**

... with **massive** clumps of **metal** hanging from her ears

a What is the name given to the sound effect used in the highlighted words?

b Do you think this type of imagery helps to make her arguments more persuasive? Why or why not?

7 How effective is the last paragraph of the article? How has the writer prepared her readers for this ending?

HINT

● Look for specific links between the ending of the article and what she writes in paragraphs 4, 5 and 6

WRITING ACTIVITY

Imagine you are a teacher who has just read Katharine Frazer-Barnes' article in the newspaper. You disagree with her views on school uniform, and you want to write a letter to the newspaper to say so. Write the first two or three paragraphs of your reply.

◆ First, think about the points in *favour* of school uniform. Include evidence and examples from your own experience.

◆ Then think about the order in which you will organize them into paragraphs, and how you will make your letter persuasive (look at the techniques used in the article).

◆ Next, think about how you will start your letter.

You could begin with one of these opening sentences:

Dear Sir/Madam

I have just read Katharine Frazer-Barnes' opinion piece on school uniform. I disagree with her views for several reasons . . .

OR

So Katharine Frazer-Barnes isn't a fan of school uniform. Most pupils aren't. My view is . . .

Advertising
Asking for Support

OBJECTIVES

These two advertisements are aimed at persuading their readers to do different things. You will study the following objectives:

- Word level: *connectives*

- Sentence level: *main point of paragraph*, *paragraph structure*, and *sentence variety*

- Reading: *media audiences* (how texts are tailored to their audience), *print, sound and image*, *non-fiction style* (how writers match language and organization to their intentions), and *language choices*

- Writing: *drafting process*, and *express a view*

Introduction

Advertising is one of the most powerful forms of persuasive writing, and one we see around us all the time. Advertisements might be used to persuade us to buy a product (e.g. a certain brand of jeans), or to change our attitude (e.g. a political advertisement asking us to vote for a certain party), or to use certain services (e.g. join an organization).

Not all advertisements use text, of course. Some use images (such as print and TV commercials); some use sound effects.

This unit contains two print advertisements. Both appeared in newspapers.

- One is persuading us to support an organization (Save the Children).

- One is promoting a product (the Barlow Knee Support).

When you have studied these advertisements, you will be able to devise one of your own.

Text A

In Huanta, Peru you don't talk to Ofsted about improving the school.

You talk to Eduardo.

Eduardo is not a schools inspector. Or a governor. Or even a teacher.

He is a pupil at one of the poorest schools in Peru. Until recently, he and most of his classmates felt the school was failing to give them the education they need. So they decided to do something about it.

With the support of Save the Children the pupils set up a school council to help improve standards. And Eduardo was voted mayor.

Now, under his leadership, the council is working closely with teachers to help bring the national curriculum to this desperately poor area. Little by little teaching standards are rising. And more children are getting the education they need to escape their poverty.

130 million children worldwide are missing out on a basic education. Helping them to improve their own schooling is just one of the ways in which Save the Children is tackling child poverty.

To find out how you can support our work during Save the Children Week, please call us on 020 7701 8916 or visit our website at www.savethechildren.org.uk

TAKE CHILDREN SERIOUSLY – HELP THEM CHANGE THE ODDS

Save the Children

Text B

At last, here's instant relief for

Knee Pain

for men and women of all ages

DO YOUR knees ache? Do they hurt every time you take a step? Do you get twinges and shooting pains every time you twist them slightly? If this sounds familiar, you are not alone. Millions of people suffer from knee pain, often caused by a bad fall, old age, a torn or worn cartilage or simply an old accident or injury. All of these are a sign of your knees crying out for proper support. Support that really works.

FOR PEOPLE OF ALL AGES!

Nothing is more excruciating than knee pain, stiffness or strain! It doesn't matter whether it comes from a sports injury, a bad twist, a fall or simply from growing older, you'd give anything for pain free relief.

The remarkable Barlow Knee Support is guaranteed to bring you immediate relief or your money back. Imagine being able to walk, climb stairs, dance, jog and enjoy life again without pain.

The Barlow Knee Support was developed by veteran football coach "Cotton" Barlow when he found ordinary knee supports and elastic bandages just didn't do the job. He set out to add strength and stability directly to the joint where support and protection are needed most.

Do you suffer from knee pain?

THREE MONTH NO-RISK TRIAL OFFER!

Order your Barlow Knee Support today and try it risk free for three whole months. We guarantee it will bring you instant relief from your knee pain – if it doesn't, we will refund you every penny of your purchase price without question.

AT LAST – NEW RELIEF FOR ALL WHO SUFFER!

The Barlow Knee Support uses no metal, yet provides you with all the maximum lateral and cap support you need. This incredibly lightweight support absorbs shocks, prevents twisting and provides soothing warmth to injured or painful joints.

© 2001, The Bristol Group Ltd, 158 Moulsham Street, Chelmsford, CM2 0LD

FREEPHONE ORDERLINE 8.30am – 10.30pm - 7 days

0800 083 0941 (ORDERLINE *ONLY*)
If you require customer service, call 023 8066 5059

Quote Dept BKS86

RETURN TO: BRISTOL GROUP, DEPT BKS86, 36 STEPHENSON ROAD, TOTTON, SOUTHAMPTON, SO40 3YD
Please send me:
☐ 1 Knee Support @ £19.95 + £3 postage and handling
☐ 2 Knee Supports @ £37.90 + £3 postage and handling
FOR CORRECT SIZE Measure around the knee, one inch above the knee cap. My exact measurement is _____ inches.
☐ I enclose a cheque/PO for £_____ payable to Bristol Group
☐ Please charge my Visa/Master/Switch card number:

EXP. DATE _____ ISSUE NO _____ SIGNATURE _____

MR/MRS/MISS/MS _____
NAME _____
ADDRESS _____

POST CODE _____

Delivery usually within one week but please allow up to 28 days. We hope to be able to bring you a variety of further interesting offers from reputable companies – if you prefer not to receive such offers, please tick this box ☐

UNDERSTANDING THE TEXT

Text A

1 Who is Eduardo?

2 Why did the children at the school want to do something?

3 How did Save the Children help in this?

Text B

4 Who invented the Barlow Knee Support?

5 What guarantee does the advertisement give?

6 Why is the trial offer at 'no risk'?

INTERPRETING THE TEXT

7 What do you think is the main aim of text A? Choose from the following:

a to help us learn about education in Peru

b to make us recognize the work Save the Children is doing

c to persuade us to send money to Save the Children

d to persuade us to visit the Save the Children website

Write a sentence explaining your answer.

8 Advertisements always have their audience firmly in mind. Who do you think the different advertisements are aimed at? Look at the images as well as the text. Use the key words below to explain your answer for each product:

general audience   *young people*   *older people*

people with a shared interest/concern   *mostly women*   *mostly men*

You might write your responses like this:

Text A seems to be aimed at _____ because …

Text B seems to be aimed at _____ because …

9 Advertisements aim to persuade us to do something. Which text do you find most persuasive, and which least persuasive? Write a brief paragraph explaining your response.

LANGUAGE AND STRUCTURE

Text A

1 Persuasive texts often start with a strong opening statement. Look at the first paragraph of the main text:

Eduardo is not a schools inspector. Or a governor. Or even a teacher.

Most writers would present this as a continuous simple sentence, like this:

Eduardo is not a schools inspector, or a governor, or even a teacher.

What effect does the writer create by breaking it into three smaller units?

2 The headline of an advertisement is vitally important in attracting the reader's attention. In this headline, the writer uses the pronoun 'you'. Instead, he could have used a noun like 'people'. What effect does using the pronoun 'you' have?

3 Look at the structure of the text. For each paragraph:

a decide what the main function of the paragraph is

b write down any connectives or linking phrases which link the paragraph back to the one before it.

Paragraph	Does it aim to persuade, appeal to its audience, inform or entertain?	Connectives / linking phrases (e.g. *and, then, gradually*)
1: 'Eduardo is …'		
2: 'He is a …'		
3: 'With the support …'		
4: 'Now …'		
5: '130 million …'		
6: 'To find out …'		

c Now write a sentence describing what you notice about how the writer has organized the text overall.

Text B

4 Persuasive texts use a range of sentences, including statements, questions, and commands.

    a Write down an example of each sentence function from the text.

    b Why do you think the writer uses questions at the beginning of the text?

    c Why do you think the writer uses a command near the end?

5 Advertisements usually aim to present a lot of information in a friendly way. The writer of text B uses subheadings throughout the text. What effect do these have?

6 Look at the structure of text B. For each paragraph:

    a decide what the main function of the paragraph is

    b write down any connectives or linking phrases which link the paragraph back to the one before it.

Paragraph	Does it aim to persuade, appeal to its audience, inform or entertain?	Connectives / linking phrases (e.g. *and, then, gradually*)
1: 'Do your knees …'		
2: 'Nothing is …'		
3: 'The remarkable …'		
4: 'The Barlow …'		
5: 'The Barlow …'		
6: 'Order …'		

    c Now write a sentence describing what you notice about how the writer has organized the text overall.

7 Adverts often use exaggerated or emotive language to describe their product. Here are some adjectives and adverbs which text B uses to describe the benefits of the Barlow Knee Support:

remarkable   immediate   incredibly   soothing

How do these words help the writer to persuade us that the product works well?

WRITING ACTIVITY

You might expect the advertisement for the Barlow Knee Support to be aimed more at people who participate in sport. How would you present the benefits of the product to an athletic, sporty audience?

◆ What image would you use?

◆ What headline would you use?

◆ How would you address the reader?

Sketch an outline to show what your advertisement would look like. Then write the first two or three paragraphs of the text.

You should:

◆ use the second person

◆ use questions

◆ use vocabulary relating to sport or athletics

◆ emphasize the reasons why the product may be useful to your target audience.

Then write a sentence describing the changes you have made to the original advertisement.

EXTENDED WRITING

Choose one of the writing challenges in the panel below. Each of them is a difficult topic. Your job is find a way of persuading your audience to agree with it. You can choose to write either an opinion piece (like the school uniform text) or an advertisement.

> ## PERSUASION TOPICS
>
> Convince your audience of school students that it would be sensible to have fewer holidays and more school time ...
>
> Convince your audience of footballers that football is a dangerous game that should be played only by professionals ...
>
> Convince your audience that the use of computers should be limited to a small amount of time per day ...

Starting points:

* Decide what arguments you will use. Think of the arguments people would make against you, so that you can build answers to these into your writing.

* Think about the features of the text type you will use (opinion piece or advertisement).

* Plan your work, perhaps brainstorming ideas with others.

Think about:

* How you will organize your ideas. Will you put the most important points first?

* How you will use vocabulary which will convince your reader.

* The sentences you will use – statements, questions, or commands? Short or long? Simple, compound or complex?

* The evidence and examples you will use.

* The links that will show how one idea follows on from another.

When you have written a few paragraphs, review them to see whether your style is really persuasive.

What is discursive writing?

Discursive writing aims to weigh up both sides of an argument. The writer usually gives her or his own opinion, but will also show what other people think.

Purpose and audience

Discursive writing is designed to present a balanced argument, often on a controversial issue. It often answers a question on a serious topic – for example, 'Is hunting cruel?'. It might be an essay, a newspaper opinion piece or a magazine article.

Text level features

The title will often be a question, or a controversial statement. The text will often be structured like this:

An **introduction** which announces the topic

Paragraphs showing different sides of the **argument**

A **conclusion** giving the writer's own view.

The writer will often make a point (an **assertion**) and then back it up with supporting **evidence** or an **example**.

Sentence level features

The text will often use the **third person** (*he/she/they*) in order to keep the tone impersonal. It might use the **first person** (*I*) when giving the writer's own opinion. The writer will use **connectives** to show how arguments are related to each other – for example: *also, similarly, in contrast, on the other hand*. Many of the sentences will be **statements**, but the writer may use **rhetorical questions** for effect – for example, 'Is this true? We need to balance the evidence . . .'

Word level features

The writer may use **emotive words** and phrases to describe strong opinions. There may be words and phrases that are used to give **structure** to arguments – *in conclusion, similarly, despite this, therefore*.

Presenting a balanced argument

Pupils' Diets a 'Disgrace'

OBJECTIVES

This text is a website page that gives different opinions on the same topic. You will study the following objectives:

- Word level: *connectives*

- Sentence level: *subordinate clauses, boundary punctuation, active and passive, starting paragraphs,* and *main point of paragraph*

- Reading: *compare presentation, identify main ideas, distinguish writer's views,* and *media audiences* (how texts are tailored to their audience)

- Writing: *planning formats, exploratory writing, present information,* and *express a view*

Introduction

News websites carry a range of information, and many people use the Internet as a main source of news. Website editors of the main news organizations therefore try to present a balanced picture – showing different viewpoints about a story.

When you have studied this discursive text, you can plan one of your own.

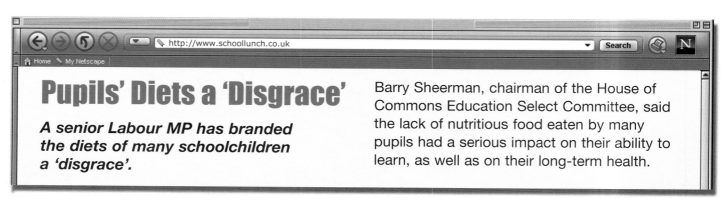

http://www.schoollunch.co.uk

Home   My Netscape

Pupils' Diets a 'Disgrace'

A senior Labour MP has branded the diets of many schoolchildren a 'disgrace'.

Barry Sheerman, chairman of the House of Commons Education Select Committee, said the lack of nutritious food eaten by many pupils had a serious impact on their ability to learn, as well as on their long-term health.

He is calling on the government to spend more money on school meals to help improve the situation.

Speaking during a Commons debate on school meals, he said: 'If they want better food, they cannot flinch from the fact that better food does mean more expense, and that means a greater budget for schools for that service.'

Last year, the government published plans to improve standards of school meals.

Labour wants to introduce new minimum legal standards for all school meals in England.

The government's new standards include proposals to ban serving baked beans in primary schools more than once a week and chips more than three times a week.

School lunch: How healthy is your child's diet?

'Vague' plans

The guidelines – due to come into force from 2001 – also say fish must be an option at least once a week, red meat not more than three times a week, and that fresh fruit should be on offer at least twice a week.

But in its report on school meals, the committee criticised the plans as vague and unworkable.

It argued that banning individual food was the wrong approach, which would do little to draw children away from junk food.

It sided with health promoters such as the National Heart Forum (NHF) which said the plans would not stop children eating pizzas, for example, whenever chips are not on the menu.

The NHF also said the plans would not stop caterers cooking so-called healthy foods in an unhealthy way.

And it believes that rules about the quantity of nutrients that people should consume would be more effective than bans on particular foods.

Free meals

During Thursday's debate, Tory MP Nick St Aubyn acknowledged that chips, beans, sausages and burgers should not be removed from school menus altogether, as children's diets had to be attractive to them as well as nutritious.

But he said: 'There can be no doubt that well-fed children, those who've had something for breakfast before they come into class, those who have nutritious food during the day, are going to be more capable of concentration on their studies.'

A number of MPs called on the government to reinstate free school meals for all pupils, to help improve children's diets and school results.

UNDERSTANDING THE TEXT

1 Who is Barry Sheerman?

2 Why does he think pupils' diets are a disgrace?

3 What do government proposals recommend for:

   a baked beans

   b fish

   c red meat?

4 What is the NHF?

5 Nick St Aubyn says chips and burgers should not be totally removed from school menus. Why?

6 Who mentions a link between children's diets and their school work?

INTERPRETING THE TEXT

7 Discursive texts usually include a number of different opinions on their topic. This text gives various views on the subject of school meals. Use a grid like this one to show what different people say:

Who	
Barry Sheerman	
The Labour government	
National Heart Forum	
Nick St Aubyn	

LANGUAGE AND STRUCTURE

1 Look at the way this web page is organized.

   a What do you notice about the way the main text is divided into paragraphs?

> ### HINTS
> - Count the number of sentences in each paragraph

   b Each sentence packs in a lot of information. Look at the one that follows the heading 'Free meals'. Where would you split this sentence, if you had to make it into two new sentences? Does putting it into a single sentence make Nick St Aubyn's argument easier or more difficult to follow?

2 Look at the headline. It could have said 'A Government committee criticizes school meals', but that doesn't sound like a headline. How does the website headline aim to catch the reader's attention?

3 Look at the first sentence of the article. It is written using the active voice, starting with the subject 'A senior Labour MP...'.

   a How would it be written in the passive voice, starting with 'The diets of many schoolchildren . . .' as the subject?

   b Does this change the effect at all?

4 Discursive texts sometimes use rhetorical questions, as in the caption beneath the image. The structure is: phrase ('School lunch'), colon (:), question.

   a What is the function of the colon here?

   b Why do you think the writer uses a question?

   c What does the question tell you about the target audience?

5 In the first sentence, the writer uses the verb 'branded'.

   a What other word might she or he have used?

   b Why do you think the verb 'branded' has been chosen?

6 Look at the sentence that follows the heading 'Vague plans'. It contains two dashes and two commas. Rewrite the sentence using another type of punctuation in place of the dashes.

> ### HINT
> • The sentence already has commas, so try something else

7 In this discursive text the writer discusses a number of different aspects of the topic in separate paragraphs, using connectives to link the paragraphs together. Find a paragraph where the writer begins with a connective showing that the following point will disagree with the previous one.

WRITING ACTIVITY

How would you design school lunch menus? What do you think the priority should be – good nutrition, or meals that students actually want?

If students are currently eating too many chips, burgers and beans, do you think that is a bad thing? Does it mean students need to be taught more about healthy eating? Should their eating habits be changed by teaching them about nutrition, or by changing what is on offer in school canteens?

Brainstorm the arguments for and against changing the menu in your school canteen, using a 2-column grid like this:

Arguments for change	Arguments against change

Try to present a balanced set of arguments.

Now write a paragraph giving your own opinion, and the reasons for it.

EXTENDED WRITING

How far do you think schools should *reflect* people's needs and behaviour?

How far do you think they should *shape* the way people behave? Look at this statement:

'Schools have a duty to teach young people. This means that they should teach them to eat healthy food and keep fit. To do this they should serve only healthy food – no sweets, no pastries, no cans of soft drink – and they should place more emphasis on compulsory sport.'

What is your first reaction? Do you agree or disagree?

Speaking and listening assignment

1   In a group, role-play a discussion in which each of you takes one of the parts below. Choose the mix of roles you would like to include in your discussion.

Some possible roles

◆   Government minister who made the statement about the duty of schools

◆   Parent who believes children should be able to choose their own food

◆   PE teacher who would like to see more emphasis on health and fitness

◆   PE teacher who thinks that a strict policy on food and fitness could turn some pupils off healthy eating and sport

◆   Representative of the National Heart Forum, trying to promote healthy lifestyles

◆   Catering company manager – worried that the company might lose money if they are not allowed to serve popular foods.

2   After your discussion, make a list of some of the different arguments that have been put forward in support of or against the proposal.

3 Describe the ways that the best speakers got their arguments across – for example, did they use jokes, or did they try to scare you into agreeing with them? Did they give convincing evidence to back up their arguments?

Essay assignment

Plan a discursive essay exploring the issue of school meals. Use this framework:

◆ start with an introduction about the statement on page 21 on the duty of schools – describe who might have made it, and why

◆ give different points of view in separate paragraphs

◆ give your own opinion in the closing paragraph.

Remember to use the following features of discursive writing:

◆ Use the third person when writing about the topic and about other people's opinions. Then use the first person if you wish, to express your own view.

◆ Aim to support the different viewpoints with appropriate evidence – e.g. give quotations or statistics.

◆ Use connectives to give structure to the different arguments – e.g. *also, in contrast, in spite of this* . . .

What are advice texts?

Purpose and audience

Advice texts aim to give us information which helps us. This means that, often, they are also persuasive texts – they aim to change our attitudes or behaviour. Often they will be addressed to a particular audience – for example, female or male readers of a magazine, or people with a special interest who are looking for advice on a topic (e.g. 'Increasing the memory in your PC'). Advice texts will sometimes share many of the features of instructions.

Text level features

The text may be organized around **questions** ('How can I best train my dog?') and it may be **illustrated** with photographs and diagrams to help give clear advice. Often it will address the reader using the **second person** ('You should start by making a list of everything that is worrying you'). Because the writer wants the reader to feel relaxed and confident about the advice, he or she will often use an **informal tone**.

Sentence level features

To make the text more informal the writer may use a **range of sentences**, including compound sentences (sentences joined by *and*, *or* or *but*). These can feel more relaxed, as if the writer is chatting to the reader. Sentence functions are likely to include **statements**, **questions** and **commands**.

Word level features

The writer will use some **description**, where it helps the reader. In general the vocabulary will be **simple** and straightforward, except where the advice is about a technical topic, in which case **technical terms** may be used. This will depend on the audience for the advice – the writer will want to use words that the reader will be familiar with, so that the advice seems reassuring and reliable.

Giving informal advice

Let's Get Physical!

OBJECTIVES

This text is a newspaper feature giving entertaining and informal advice to readers. You will be studying the following objectives:

- Word level: *subject vocabulary*

- Sentence level: *main point of paragraph*, and *sentence variety*

- Reading: *extract information*, *evaluate sources*, *active reading*, *media audiences* (how media texts are tailored to their audiences), and *print, sound and image*

- Writing: *organize texts appropriately*, *present information*, and *informal advice*

Introduction

Newspapers and magazines often contain advice pages. This feature article is taken from a newspaper aimed at young readers. It is called the *Indy* and it was published by the *Independent* newspaper. This feature gives readers advice on spotting the 'secret signs' of body language. When you have studied it, you can try writing an advice page yourself.

Let's Get Physical!

You may be saying one thing, but your body will be saying another. **Louise Osmond** *and* **Phil Cool** *on the grammar of body language*

IMAGINE THE scene: you are at a party, you are attracted to someone, you want to make a move but you are afraid of being rejected. Does this sound familiar? Well, forget the sickly smile and sweaty palms. Body watching is your answer.

As a rule, people concentrate so hard on what they're saying that they forget that their movements, gestures and expressions are telling a story of their own. Body language can tell you what mood someone's in, what they're afraid of and just how interested in you they are.

Albert Mehrabian, author of Silent Messages, suggests that we can understand more about a person if we listen to their body language than we can if we listen to their voice.

Here is a basic body language survival kit. But remember, it's important not to read body gestures in isolation. Look for a collection of gestures; a combination of body signs that will add up to give you a general impression of your subject.

Seeing eye to eye:

THE FIRST and most crucial rule is to watch people's eyes. Eyes give out the most accurate and revealing of all the body's signals.

The pupils of the eyes dilate according to mood. They expand to up to four times their normal size when you're excited and reduce to tiny black dots when you're angry.

If you sense someone might be lying, watch their eyes. People who are lying will make eye contact for less than a third of the normal time (which is sixty or seventy per cent) and will look down or away from you as they speak.

Staring:

WHEN SOMEONE gazes intensely into your eyes it means one of two things:

Either he/she finds you very interesting or appealing, in which case their pupils will be big and fruity. Good news. Or else he/she is hostile to you and may be issuing a silent challenge. In this case the pupils will be constricted. Beware.

Arms and legs:

WATCH WHAT people do with their arms and legs. You will often find that someone with one or both arms folded across their body is in a nervous or negative mood, even if they are not conscious of it.

People disguise the building of arm barriers in any number of ways – pretending to wind up a watch, for example, or adjusting a bracelet, or simply fiddling with a sleeve.

Legs:

THIS IS a useful one to know at parties. Legs can tell you a lot about someone, particularly when their owner is standing up.

People often stand in groups at parties. If a member of the group has their legs and arms crossed, they are probably standing with strangers and wishing they could go home.

A person standing among friends looks very different. Their arms are relaxed and their palms are open. The open palms say: 'I've got nothing to hide, take from me what you want.' They are a sign of honesty.

Relaxed people lean on one foot and point the other towards anyone in the group they like or are attracted to.

Sitting down:

CROSSED LEGS should be read with care. Girls are taught from an early age that it is more 'lady-like' to sit down with crossed legs, and this can confuse things.

Luckily, the direction of the upper leg gives some clue to the person's mood. If the upper knee is pointing away from you it probably means something negative. If, however, the knee is pointing towards you, you may be on to a good thing. It could be a sign of positive interest.

Imitation:

COPYING SOMEONE'S gestures during a conversation is a sign of interest, agreement, or even affection. It's a sub-conscious instinct.

The sociologist Schleflen found that strangers often carefully avoid holding the same positions. But if they start to hit it off together, they will begin to perform a little pageant, tilting their heads at each other and crossing and uncrossing their legs in happy unison.

Deliberately mirroring someone can be a good way of putting them at their ease.

UNDERSTANDING THE TEXT

1 According to the first two paragraphs, what can body language tell you about a person?

2 Why is watching someone's eyes the most important rule?

3 What might it mean if someone imitates your body language?

INTERPRETING THE TEXT

4 Look more closely at the first paragraph. How does the writer try to hook the reader's interest in the topic?

5 Advice texts are often illustrated. What does the photograph used here add to the article overall? Does it:

a help the reader to understand the article?

b make the article more serious?

c make the article less serious?

d demonstrate some specific examples?

Choose the statement you most agree with and write a sentence or two explaining your choice.

6 Which parts of the body language advice do you find convincing? Are there parts you do not agree with? Write a brief paragraph giving your response to the text, and saying how valuable you think its advice is.

7 Advice texts can use a lot of description to help the reader. Re-read the text, and concentrate on visualizing the body language it is describing as you read. Does this technique help you to remember the main points of the article? After reading, write down as many points as you can remember.

8 How can you tell from the language used that the article is aimed at young people? Write down some examples to support your answer.

LANGUAGE AND STRUCTURE

1 The text uses subheadings to organize the advice and information. The first four paragraphs do not have a subheading. How would you sum up what they are about? Try to find one word or phrase which could serve as a subheading for all of these paragraphs.

2 a Quickly scan the text to see how many different categories of body language it describes.

   b How would this task have been different if the text did not have subheadings?

3 Some advice texts use technical words that are suitable for their topic. This text says: 'The pupils of the eyes dilate'. Decide on another word or phrase that could be used instead of 'dilate'.

4 Advice texts often use command sentences, usually starting with imperative verbs, and directly addressing the reader: 'Imagine the scene . . .'

Look at paragraph 4, and write down the beginning of another command.

5 The writer uses a range of styles. Some are factual; some offer advice. Look at these sentences and, for each one, say whether it is fact (F) or advice (A). Then write down the main clue that helped you to decide:

   a *If you sense someone might be lying, watch their eyes.*

   b *A person standing among friends looks very different.*

   c *Crossed legs should be read with care.*

   d *Deliberately mirroring someone can be a good way of putting them at their ease.*

6 Advice texts are often written in an informal style. Look at this sentence:

Body language can tell you what mood someone's in, what they're afraid of and just how interested in you they are.

   a In what ways does the writer's style seem quite informal?

   b Rewrite the sentence in a more formal way, so that it feels less chatty.

7 Advice texts often support their main points with examples, to help the reader. Find a place in this text where a sentence giving general information is followed by a sentence offering an example.

WRITING ACTIVITY

Imagine you are writing an advice page for people who have not read this article. It will appear in a teenage magazine. Your piece is called 'How to know if she/he really likes you'. Using some of the information from the *Independent* article, write down five main hints on the signs that someone should look for.

◆ Organize your points into a suitable order.

◆ Write your text as advice, rather than in a factual style.

◆ Remember to use imperative verbs ('look out for . . .')

◆ Remember to address you reader directly ('you . . .')

◆ Imagine your audience is the same sex as you (i.e. girls write to girls, and boys write to boys)

◆ Vary the structure of your sentences. You might want to use some conditional clauses: 'If he . . . then he probably . . .'

You might start like this.

New Kid on the Block

Someone new just walked into your tutor group? How will you know what he/she thinks about you? Here's some advice . . .

First . . .

Next . . .

29

EXTENDED WRITING

Choose a topic you know a lot about, and write an advice sheet for a general reader.

Think of a title which begins 'How to . . .'

Some possible topics:

◆ How to win at . . . [name of a computer game]

◆ How to learn to skateboard

◆ How to improve your soccer skills

◆ How to write better stories.

Consider your audience. They don't know as much as you do about the topic – but they are interested.

◆ Think about the vocabulary you will choose. Will you use technical words?

◆ Think about how you will address the reader.

◆ Think of ways to communicate your advice clearly – for example by using subheadings, diagrams, charts, a glossary of technical terms, or a separate 'hints panel'.

Start by planning the information you will use, including the 'How to . . .' heading. Then plan the layout of your advice sheet, and write the text (one side of A4 paper only).

What is an evaluation?

Purpose and audience

Evaluations aim to discuss the strengths and weaknesses of something. It might be a play, a book we have read, or a process – such as a technology project or science experiment. We sometimes write evaluations for our own use: they help us to reflect on what we did well and what we need to improve (e.g. setting personal targets in school reports). Other evaluations are used for assessment by others – for example, to show how well we have understood a process, like a science experiment.

Text level features

The title may ask a **question**: 'What have I learnt?' 'How well did the process work?' Writers might use **layout features** such as a table to list strengths and weaknesses, or bullet points.

Sentence level features

Evaluations will often be written in the **third person**. But even in an impersonal text, an evaluation section may be more personal, using the **first person** (I) to give a personal opinion. Evaluations will usually be written in the **past tense**. They will use **connectives** to organize points: *although, however, therefore, this shows that.* The best evaluations will avoid bland, meaningless comments such as 'I wasn't very good', and will give precise **detail**.

Word level features

The writer will use **technical terms**. She or he will include vocabulary that is related to **comment** – for example, 'I thought… I expected . . . I learnt that . . .'.

4 Writing an evaluation
Science Experiment

Introduction

In subjects like science and technology you will often be asked to evaluate a process. This usually forms the final part of an assignment. The example given here was written by Tom Fullam, a student in Suffolk. It is part of his report of a science experiment. The final section shows how he approached the evaluation. When you have read his work, you will be able to write your own version of his evaluation.

Science Experiment

Aim: To investigate the effect of different colours on the rate of cooling of water.

Introduction: We did a preliminary experiment involving only two colours, matt black and silver foil.

We carried out a preliminary experiment, where we measured the temperature change over 10 minutes in two test tubes of hot water (75°C) as they cooled. One was covered with foil, and one was covered with black paper.

The foil covered tube cooled by 18°C.
The black paper covered tube cooled by 21°C.

Dull black surfaces are the best absorbers of radiation. They reflect hardly any radiation at all.

Shiny silver surfaces are the worst absorbers of radiation. They reflect nearly all the radiation that strikes them

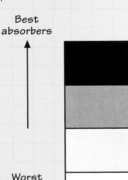 

Best absorbers

Worst absorbers

Best emitters

Worst emitters

Dull black surfaces are the best emitters of radiation.

Silvery surfaces are the worst emitters of radiation.

Hypothesis: I predict that the water in the boiling tube covered in black paper will cool the quickest. This is because the black outer surface will radiate the heat into the air in the room, while the surface inside the tube will absorb the heat well.

The silver foil covered test tube will cool the slowest, because its silvery surface will not absorb the heat radiation well. Also, because the outer surface is also silvery, the heat that does get absorbed will not be radiated effectively into the room.

The white paper covered tube is not as good at absorbing and radiating heat as the black paper, but it is better than the silver.

Apparatus:

4 Boiling tubes	Test tube rack
Black paper	Goggles
Silver foil	Kettle (to supply the hot water)
White paper	Cotton wool (to use in absence of a rubber bung)
Timer	Thermometer

To ensure a fair test, the width and layers of the foil and paper must be as equal as possible. The test will last 15 minutes, to get a well-spread set of results, and the experiment will be repeated 3 times, for the same reasons.

Method
- For safety, goggles will be worn.
- Cover a boiling tube with black paper, another tube with white paper, another with foil, and the last tube is left alone (as a control). Make sure only one layer of paper/foil is put on each appropriate boiling tube.
- Measure out freshly boiled water into 4 equal 35cm^3 amounts.
- Put the test tubes into the test tube rack, and pour the 35cm^3 measures of water into each tube.
- Put the thermometers into each tube, and let them rest on the bottom of the tube.
- Plug the hole in the top of the tubes with equal amounts of cotton wool.
- When the temperature has levelled out (after several seconds) start recording the temperatures (every minute, for 15 minutes, including the starting temperature at minute 0).
- Repeat the experiment 3 times to get an average.

Fair test

The following things will be done to make sure that the experiment is a fair test.
- The temperature on the thermometers must have settled before the timers are started, as there is a small amount of inaccuracy.
- The height of the thermometers will be the same, because convection currents may make the temperature different if the thermometer rests higher or lower.
- The boiling tubes will all be the same size, then they will have the same surface area. The surface area affects the cooling rate of the water.
- One layer of paper/foil will be used. If there are more layers wrapped around the tube, then they could trap unequal amounts of air (to form insulation).
- The kettle will be freshly boiled each time, to keep the starting temperatures the same.

Results:

Time in minutes	Black temp (°)	White temp (°)	Foil temp (°)	Control temp (°)
0	60	60	60	60
1	58	58	57	57
2	56	56	55	55
3	55	55	53	53
4	54	53	52	51
5	52	52	50	49
6	51	51	48	47
7	49	49	46	46
8	48	49	46	44
9	47	47	45	43
10	46	46	44	42
11	45	45	42	40
12	44	44	42	39
13	43	43	41	38
14	43	43	40	38
15	42	41	39	37

Conclusion: The results of the experiment seemed to indicate that matt black was the better colour, even though my prediction and various text books stated otherwise. The evidence of this being incorrect is also shown by the fact that there seemed to be no major differences between the temperatures the materials kept the water at, with only an average range of 5. However, since the control tube had the lowest temperature, this indicates that surfaces of differing radiating abilities all had a positive effect on the water temperature-cooling rate. Tin foil SHOULD have kept the highest temperature, but it appeared to be the second lowest.

Evaluation: Although I did not notice anything go drastically wrong with the experiment, there seemed to be an incorrect result to it, with the black paper seemingly better at retaining heat. Several factors could have made this possible. The cotton wool we used to bung the test-tubes was varying in thickness, so the black paper could have had a thick wedge, while the silver foil could have had a thinner one, allowing more heat to escape. Also, the test tubes had the hot water added to them in the same order, so by the time it had reached the silver foil encased tube, it could have marginally cooled down, changing our results. Also, the black paper was thicker than the silver foil, so it could work as a better insulator. These factors made the experiment unfair. If I could repeat the experiment, I would use proper rubber bungs of equal density, and use four kettles (something that was not possible when we did the experiment). This would have made the information both more reliable and more accurate.

UNDERSTANDING THE TEXT

1 In your own words, describe what the experiment is designed to find out.

2 What did Tom Fullam predict would be the result?

3 What surprised him about the result?

4 Give one clue from the text that Tom Fullam has paid attention to safety issues.

5 Scan the text to find:

a how many things were done to make sure the experiment was a fair test

b the time in minutes that it took the 'control' test tube to cool to 49°.

INTERPRETING THE TEXT

6 What do you learn from the diagram Tom uses? Do you learn anything from the diagram and labels that is not mentioned in the text?

7 How can you tell that the text is aimed at a specialist audience – readers who already know something about science experiments?

HINTS

- Look at the vocabulary Tom chooses
- Look at the subheadings he uses to organize his text

8 What does his 'Evaluation' section show Tom has learnt from the experiment?

9 Re-read Tom's 'Hypothesis' section. Now complete the following sentences, comparing what he predicts about the different test tubes:

The test tube covered in . . . will cool most quickly.

The test tube covered in . . . will cool more slowly than this.

The test tube covered in . . . will cool most slowly of all.

LANGUAGE AND STRUCTURE

1 Evaluations use a range of layout features to help make the information clear, including subheadings.

 a How do the subheadings in this text help the reader?

 b Under his subheadings, does Tom organize his paragraphs well, or are any of them too long or too short? Explain your answer.

2 In some places, the writer uses the present tense; in some he uses the past; and in others he uses the future tense.

 Look at the sentences below. For each one say which tense Tom Fullam is using and why you think he does this.

Example	Tense	Reason
We did a preliminary experiment involving only two colours		
The silver foil covered test tube will cool the slowest		
The white paper covered tube is not as good at absorbing and radiating heat as the black paper, but it is better than the silver.		

3 a What tense would you expect the writer to use for an evaluation?

b Does Tom use this tense throughout his 'Evaluation' section? If not, why not?

4 Tom Fullam uses the passive voice in parts of his assignment. For each of the examples below, write down how they could be written in the active voice:

Passive version	Active version
For safety, goggles will be worn	
The kettle will be freshly boiled each time	
The test tubes had the hot water added to them	

5 In his conclusion and evaluation sections, Tom uses a number of connectives to join his ideas together. Write down three connectives he uses.

6 Evaluations often use technical or specialist terms. Write down three examples of technical words that Tom Fullam uses. For each one, try to think of an everyday word that means something similar.

WRITING ACTIVITY

Tom Fullam's assignment is written in quite a formal style. His words would be very different if he was just chatting to a friend after doing the experiment.

His friend asks what he did last lesson, and Tom briefly describes the experiment. How would his use of language be different from the formal assignment? Write part of Tom's spoken account, using words and structures that we find in spoken language. You could start like this:

Friend: So what were you doing last lesson?

Tom: Well, we were doing an experiment to try and find out how …

Your account should include Tom's evaluation of whether the experiment went well or badly, and why.

When you have finished, write a sentence describing the main ways in which your spoken version differs from the text written by Tom.

Writing a review
Harry Potter

Introduction

Reviews appear in magazines and newspapers and on websites. They aim to evaluate the quality of different products – from new cars to plays and films, books, even the food in restaurants.

A reviewer usually describes the features of the book, play or film he or she is reviewing, and then evaluates how successful it is.

Reviews share many of the features of evaluations (see page 31), but often use the first and second person to give personal views and to address the reader directly. They are often written in the present tense.

The following texts are two book reviews, one written by pupil Sam Flintham-Ward in Year 8. This apeared in *English and Media* magazine, and reviews *Harry Potter and the Prisoner of Azkaban*. The second is by India Knight, a writer in the *Sunday Times*, reviewing *Harry Potter and the Goblet of Fire*. When you have read these reviews you can write about the different opinions they express.

Text A

Harry Potter

This latest Harry Potter book, like the previous two, is guaranteed to grab any child or adult. Instantly, it will transport them to the world of Hogwarts, the school of witchcraft and wizardry.

Rowling's characters vary enormously. In the book we become fascinated and terrified by the Dementors and intrigued by the mysterious Professor Lupin. We become more attached to the regular characters, the loveable Hagrid, loyal Ron and the hardworking Hermione. But it's not all happy families: Rowling develops the characters of Draco Malfoy, a sly and detestable lad who has it in for Harry; Uncle Vernon, Aunt Petunia and Dudley, Harry's closest family, who make his life intolerable.

Woven into the plot of the escaped prisoner, Sirius Black, we become increasingly inquisitive to know more from the mysterious classes of the Defence Against the Arts and Hagrid's Magical Creatures. The 'Quidditch' matches provide entertainment which can be described as just as significant to the Hogwarts' students as the FA cup may be to the reader.

Rowling writes so that you can actually visualise each situation, feel the emotions, from anxiety to amazing joy, and participate in the story. She combines humorous moments with real life situations; twists are often introduced which make the book quite addictive.

Every chapter is packed full of original adventures which constantly surprise the reader. The third Harry Potter book has its own ideas and stands alone as an excellent book, regardless of whether you have read the others in the series. It's a terrific holiday read – if you can wait that long!

Sam Flintham-Ward, Year 8

Text B

HARRY IS TOO HORRIBLE

LAST SATURDAY MORNING SAW MY seven-year-old son, his nine-year-old friend and myself all hanging about the letter box in our pyjamas, hopping up and down with excitement. We were, of course, waiting for *Harry Potter and the Goblet of Fire*, pre-ordered from Amazon months ago.

As soon as it arrived – 'Harry Potter?' said the postman, knowingly - I grabbed it from two pairs of excited little hands and informed the children that we'd read the book in tandem, me in the daytime and them, out loud to each other, at bedtime. Then I left the children downstairs, got back into bed, and started reading.

As the reviewers will tell you, the fourth Harry Potter is as enchanting and compulsive as the others, if not more so. But it is also very dark indeed - darker even than its predecessor, *Harry Potter and the Prisoner of Azkaban*.

That book featured tall, cold, hooded creatures called the Dementors. They had no faces and sucked the life force from people, or sent them mad in the most graphic and distressing way. This new book makes the Dementors look like Flopsy Bunnies: it kicks off with three unsolved killings and swiftly moves on to describe a creature so evil and freakishly deformed - or rather, unformed - that an old man dies of fright just from looking at it. All in chapter one.

This is the point at which I started to wonder whether *Harry Potter and the Goblet of Fire* was suitable reading material for my seven-year-old. To be fair to J. K. Rowling, the books are not, and never were, written for such young children; they are aimed at 9 to 11-year-olds (Harry Potter himself is now 14, as, presumably, are many of his readers who have grown up alongside the books).

Unfortunately, the hype and hysteria surrounding publication of Potter is such that every child in the country is aware of the new book's existence, and longing to read it or have it read to them.

By Saturday lunchtime, I was fairly certain that I didn't want my children reading *Goblet of Fire*. But the book was in the house, the boys were begging to have a go, and so, against my instinct, I handed it to them at bedtime.

Everything went very quiet for an hour or so, then they appeared in the living room, white and scared out of their wits. My son's friend, visiting from Glasgow, is not a child you'd call wet, unless you fancied a kick in the teeth.

But even he asked to have the light left on.

It is, of course, within our natures to enjoy the thrill of being terrified. One of the many admirable things about the Harry Potter series is that the author recognises this and, in the other books, plays it just right: the horror remains on the right side of nightmarish. This time around, though, as I discovered when I hit chapter 32, the horror is hard-core. Here's an example: 'The thing had the shape of a crouched human child, except that Harry had never seen anything less like a child. It was hairless and scaly looking, a dark, raw, reddish black. Its arms and legs were thin and feeble, and its face - no child alive ever had a face like that - was flat and snakelike, with gleaming red eyes.'

This passage is followed by the creature performing an act of self-amputation, then a blood-letting ritual. I don't mind telling you that, aged $34\frac{1}{2}$, I felt really creeped out reading this in a creaky house at 2am.

I bow to no one in my admiration of Joanne Rowling, particularly for her enormous new house in Kensington. I also think it's a disgrace, for example, that she didn't win the Whitbread prize last year. But we should be wary of the lazy comparisons made between her work and that of others. Bandying her name about in the same breath as that of authors such as C. S. Lewis, Arthur Ransome or even Roald Dahl suggests her books are sweet, jolly - or, in the case of Lewis, comfortingly Christian - romps, which any vaguely literate child would enjoy.

This is not the case. The Potter books are dark and getting darker. This is one of their strengths: though moral, the books are also complex, in an unpatronising way that's a breath of fresh air when it comes to children's literature.

But I do feel it's a shame that all the little jokes and wonderful depictions of wizard life - real garden gnomes that run about squealing, house elves getting excited about owning socks, thrilling fights against dragons, half-giantesses in denial about their ancestry - should be out of bounds to my children for the next couple of years because so much of this book is plain scary.

Explaining to my son that he could not read the book was a nightmare and, given his interest, felt unfair. Surely Bloomsbury, Rowling's publisher, has a duty to market the book responsibly, rather than target every child in the country regardless of age?

Do enjoy the book, and do buy it for your children - but if they are under nine, or easily scared, read it yourself first.

India Knight

UNDERSTANDING THE TEXT

Text A

1 In paragraph 2 the writer mentions some new characters who appear in this book. Who are they?

2 Name two things that the writer likes about the book.

3 Does he name anything that he does not like?

Text B

4 Why is everyone so excited in the first paragraph?

5 Name two things that the writer likes about the novel.

6 What does she not like about it?

7 What is the main point writer B makes about J. K. Rowling's publishers?

INTERPRETING THE TEXT

8 When the writer in text B says that the book is 'very dark indeed', what does she mean by 'dark'?

9 Who do you think is the audience for text A? How can you tell? Who do you think is the audience for text B?

LANGUAGE AND STRUCTURE

1 Text A has five paragraphs. Describe the structure of the review by saying in one word or phrase what each paragraph is about, like this:

Paragraph	What it is about
1: 'This latest …'	
2: 'Rowling's …'	
3: 'Woven into …'	
4: 'Rowling writes …'	
5: 'Every chapter …'	

2 Reviews usually give personal opinions, and the writer of text A gives plenty of personal opinions about the book. Write down an example of a sentence which shows an opinion.

3 The intention of writer A seems to be to persuade other people to read the book. How successful is he in this? Give examples of sentences that you find persuasive, or not persuasive enough!

4 Writer B says:

My son's friend, visiting from Glasgow, is not a child you'd call wet, unless you fancied a kick in the teeth.

a What does she mean? What characteristics can you infer (work out from the text) that the friend has?

b How could she have written the idea in a more straightforward way?

c Why do you think she writes it in the way she does? What effect is she trying to create?

5 Writer B also writes:

I don't mind telling you that, aged $34\frac{1}{2}$, I felt really creeped out reading this in a creaky house at 2am.

a Think of a different word she might have used instead of the phrase 'creeped out'.

b Would your chosen word be better than 'creeped out'? Explain why or why not.

6 Look at the last two paragraphs of text B again:

Explaining to my son that he could not read the book was a nightmare and, given his interest, felt unfair. (1) *Surely Bloomsbury, Rowling's publisher, has a duty to market the book responsibly, rather than target every child in the country regardless of age?* (2)

Do enjoy the book, and do buy it for your children – but if they are under nine, or easily scared, read it yourself first. (3)

a Using the numbers 1-3, write down which of these sentences is a question, which is a command and which is a statement.

b Why do you think the writer uses this variety of sentence functions? What effect does it have?

c Why do you think the writer begins a new paragraph for sentence 3?

WRITING ACTIVITY

Writer A is enthusiastic in his book review. Writer B worries about the effect the book might have. Imagine writers A and B having a conversation about *Harry Potter* books. Writer A argues that children aged 7 and above will enjoy the books if an adult reads to them; writer B says that it is irresponsible for the books to be marketed at children so young.

a In pairs, have a conversation, putting these points and trying to reach an agreement. You might start like this:

A: I just read your review and I don't think it's very fair.

B: Why not?

A: Well, for a start . . .

b Write down the conversation, either as a transcript of what the two speakers might say, or by imagining that it is an e-mail exchange between them. You might start like this:

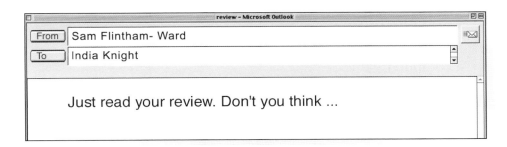

review – Microsoft Outlook

| From | Sam Flintham- Ward |
| To | India Knight |

Just read your review. Don't you think ...

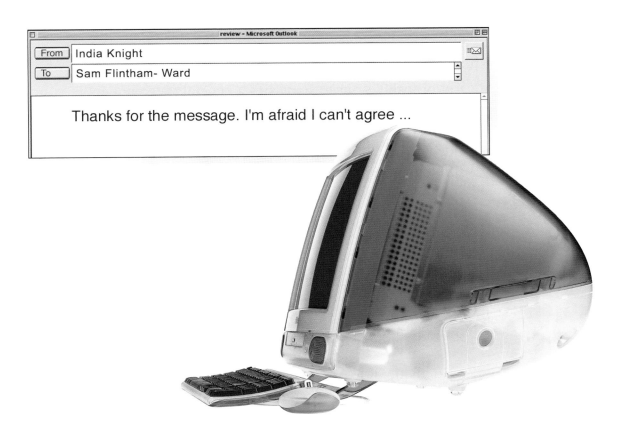

review – Microsoft Outlook

| From | India Knight |
| To | Sam Flintham- Ward |

Thanks for the message. I'm afraid I can't agree ...

EXTENDED WRITING

Write a review of something you have recently seen, read or experienced.

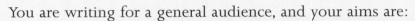

You might choose:

- a book
- a magazine
- a CD
- a play, film or TV programme
- a meal (including one you ate at school)
- a computer game.

You are writing for a general audience, and your aims are:

- to give detailed information about your subject – what it involves (you might mention characters, music, animations, language, pace, structure . . . as appropriate)
- to tell them how good it is.

Think about the structure of your review.

- You probably want to start with a general statement about your subject (e.g. 'This is the latest release . . .') or information about who it is by.
- Then you might use a number of paragraphs to focus on different aspects (features) of your subject (e.g. for a book review you would want to discuss characters, plot, setting, and language).
- Finally, you will want to give an evaluation of your subject, using adjectives which show your opinion (*successful, fast-paced, boring, tense, enjoyable, well-crafted, unoriginal, predictable* . . .)

Remember to:

- find ways of keeping the reader interested (e.g. vary your sentences)
- avoid saying 'I' too much
- use the present tense, mostly
- give specific examples, including quotations, where possible.

Persuasive writing: the essentials

Purpose and audience

Persuasive writing aims to:

- express a point of view
- change your opinions
- get you to buy something.

Text types used for persuasive writing include letters, essays, advertisements, leaflets, television programmes, newspaper editorials and opinion pieces. Writers will use language and structures intended to make you see things from their point of view.

Text level features

- The text may use **illustrations** to help get its points across.
- It may use **layout features** – such as font sizes – for impact.
- The writing may start with an **opening statement**, and then go through **key points** in more detail.
- **Logical links** will guide readers through the points made.
- The writer may use **humour** to catch the reader's interest.

Sentence level features

- The writer may use the **first person** (I, me, we) to express opinions, or may write using the **third person** (she, he, they) for a more impersonal effect.
- Advertising might use the **second person** and **imperatives** (commands) to create a more direct appeal.
- Persuasive writing will usually use **active** rather than passive sentence structures, and is often written in the **present tense**.

Word level features

- **Emotive words** may be chosen to try to influence the reader, and sometimes **exaggerated language**.
- In advertising, writers may use **word play** for effect.

5 Getting your point across

It's For You

Introduction

Here is an opinion piece by a teacher at a sixth form college. She wrote this article in a newspaper aimed at new teachers. Her purpose is to show the effects mobile phones can have on your lessons if you are a teacher. See whether you think she presents a persuasive argument. When you have studied this text, you can write a persuasive article of your own.

GLOSSARY

winsome – *pleasing or attractive*

It's for you

The mobile phone is a menace to even the best-planned class.
Cassandra Hilland has heard one bleep too many

Imagine it's your first proper lesson. It has to go well. You worry you'll be scarred for life if it doesn't. So you've planned and agonised over acetates, dithered over delivery, and decided that your bum does look big in your new trouser suit. Finally, you're ready (you hope). It's 9am, time for the first lesson of the rest of your life.

By 9.20, you're in full flow. Your punchy opening grabbed their interest. Your pitch was spot on. Now you're gliding through your audio-visuals with the winsome grace of a weather girl. As you remember their names and ask questions, you think you're the best teacher in the stratosphere. Now you're going to deconstruct Hamlet's language. You fix the class with an intense stare: 'Right then. Let us consider the character of this complex individual.' (God you're good!) 'What do you think Hamlet meant by his last words: "The rest is silence?" Hmmmm?'

You pause for dramatic effect. Then a mobile phone starts to bleep. While you try to recapture your lost chain of thought, every student in the class rummages in pockets and bags. Before they were focused, now they're wriggling in their seats. You have changed from Impressive Teacher into Flailing Failure in nanoseconds.

The lesson is trashed. All you can hear are giggles and a tacky rendition of 'Greensleeves'. Forget what they told you about disruptive pupils – the real threat to discipline is the mobile phone.

My response is to paste a large sign on my classroom door requesting that mobile phones be switched off before entering. The day after the warning goes up, a pulse trills from a girl's bag. I snarl. 'It's okay,' she reassures me. 'It's my pager, not my mobile!' The class laughs uneasily. I wince. What other digital demons have I left out? This may cause amusement, but it is a waste of teaching time.

These communication aids actually achieve the opposite. They not only distract but initiate battles of one-upmanship and anti-social behaviour. There we are discussing poetry when, suddenly, the affable young chap who's just been so articulate on symbolism has turned his back and is grunting into a plastic box. Worse is the bizarre status students attach to mobiles. Students even assert their group identity through a chosen make and model. For example, there's a chrome Samsung number which is so expensive that any student who

owns one is sending out a clear signal to their peers.

The student mobile phone user is a sign of changing times. I don't understand voice dialling, or press-on covers, and most of these little gimmicks are harmless. But there are some altogether more sinister aspects to mobile phone use that are only just being uncovered.

Text message bullying is a problem. So is cheating. Now that the latest phones can access the Internet, students can search for answers. Perhaps we will have to frisk tomorrow's students for gadgets before they

sit their exams. Or use an airport-style sensor at the exam hall door.

In the absence of any solution in the battle to stop students using mobiles in the classroom, I suggest the following: lay down the law from day one. Get your students into the habit of switching off phones, pagers and car alarms before they enter the classroom. You could even have a fish tank of piranhas on your desk, with some fluorescent-fronted phones at the bottom as a thought-provoking decoration.

As for me, I've taken the ultimate precaution – lining my classroom walls with lead.

UNDERSTANDING THE TEXT

1 Look at the first paragraph. Who do you think the writer is addressing here?

2 What words and phrases in paragraph 2 suggest that the imaginary lesson is going well?

3 Look at paragraph 4: 'Forget what they told you about disruptive pupils . . .' . Who do you think 'they' refers to?

4 What does the writer mean by 'the bizarre status pupils attach to mobile phones' (paragraph 6)?

5 What is the writer's advice for dealing with mobile phones in class?

INTERPRETING THE TEXT

6 What impression do you gain of the writer's personality from the text? Give reasons for your answer.

7 Persuasive texts often include humour. How does this writer use humour to make her points? Look for examples of:

- ◆ deliberate exaggeration
- ◆ poking fun at teachers and pupils
- ◆ comic phrases
- ◆ telling a story.

8 Some readers may feel that the writer is not objective enough – that she makes **assertions** (opinionated comments) without supporting them with evidence. Is this true? Find an example from the text as evidence for your view.

9 Which parts of the writer's article do you agree with? Which do you disagree with? Working in pairs or a small group, argue the case for and against pupils having mobile phones in school. Try to come up with a list of arguments for and against their use. You could do this in role – one of you playing the part of a pupil, another a parent, another a teacher, another could be someone from a mobile phone company.

UNIT 5

LANGUAGE AND STRUCTURE

1 a Look at the way the writer uses the first-person (*I* and *we*) and the second-person (*you*) forms to give her opinion. Which paragraphs use the first person and which use the second?

Paragraph	First or second person?
1: 'Imagine ...'	
2: 'By 9.20 ...'	
3: 'You pause ...'	
4: 'The lesson ...'	
5: 'My response ...'	
6: 'These communication ...'	
7: 'The student ...'	
8: 'Text message ...'	
9: 'In the absence ...'	
10: 'As for me ···'	

b Why do you think the writer uses the second-person form? How does it help her to make her article comic?

2 If the writer had written the article only in the first-person form, how would it have sounded?

a Rewrite the first paragraph in the first person, starting like this:

Imagine my first proper lesson . . .

b Comment on any problems you faced in changing the paragraph to the first person.

3 a The writer uses some very short sentences:

The lesson is trashed.

I wince.

Find some more examples of simple sentences like these, and describe the effect they have on the reader.

b Using simple sentences like these is one way in which the writer makes her style informal. Another is the vocabulary she chooses, e.g. writing *trashed* instead of *ruined*. Take the following informal sentences and rewrite them in a more formal style. Choose more formal vocabulary and try using the third person, the past tense and a passive structure. The first person is done for you.

Informal	**Formal**
All you can hear are giggles . . .	*All that could be heard was laughter . . .*
Your punchy opening grabbed their interest.	
Get your students into the habit of switching off phones.	

4 The writer uses the present tense throughout her article. Instead, she might have written it in the first person using the past tense: *By 9.20 I was in full flow.*

Why do you think she uses the present tense? What effect does it have?

5 Persuasive texts sometimes use commands. Why does this writer use commands (look at the last-but-one paragraph)?

WRITING ACTIVITY

Some readers may feel that the writer gives a very one-sided view of mobile phones. Write a short response as a student, stating the case for mobile phones and why, used sensibly, they are valuable for students to have. Use a similar style to the writer's – that is, use the present tense and the second person. You might start like this:

Imagine you are a student. You are travelling to school. You realize you have left something vital at home . . .

Continue this text to make a strong case in favour of mobile phones. Develop your arguments in a way that is logical for the reader to follow.

Marketing
Improving Your Memory

OBJECTIVES

These texts are both aiming to market an idea. These are the objectives you will be studying:

- Word level: *words in context*
- Sentence level: *variety of sentence structure, grouping sentences (into paragraphs), cohesion and coherence, adapting text types,* and *degrees of formality*
- Reading: *trace developments* (of themes and ideas), and *development of key ideas*
- Writing: *present a case persuasively*, and *develop an argument*

Introduction

These two persuasive texts are about ways to improve your memory. The first is an advertisement that appeared in the *Independent* newspaper in 1997. The second is an American website which aims to persuade people that they could make better use of their memories.

The two texts use very different approaches. When you have studied them, you can write an advertisement of your own.

GLOSSARY

feat – *achievement*

Text A

A Startling Memory Feat That You Can Do

How I learned the secret in one evening. It has helped me every day.

When my old friend Richard Faulkner invited me to a dinner party at his house, I little thought it would be the direct means of doubling my salary in less than two years.

Towards the end of the evening things began to drag a bit as they often do at parties. Finally someone suggested the old idea of having everyone do a 'party-piece'.

When it came to Peter Brown's turn, he said he had a simple 'trick' which he hoped we would like. First he asked to be blindfolded. Then he asked someone to shuffle a deck of cards and call them out in order. Still blindfolded he instantly named the cards in their order backwards and forwards without making a single mistake.

You may well imagine our amazement at Peter's remarkable memory feat.

On the way home that evening I asked Peter Brown how it was done. He said there was really nothing to it – simply a memory feat. Anyone could develop a good memory, he said, by following a few simple rules. And then he told me exactly how to do it.

What Peter said I took to heart. In one evening I made remarkable strides towards improving my memory. In just a few days I learned to do exactly what he had done.

The most gratifying thing about the improvement of my memory was the remarkable way it helped me in business and in my social life. I discovered that my memory training had literally put a razor edge on my mind. My thinking had become clearer, quicker, keener.

Then I noticed a marked improvement in my writing and conversational powers. What's more my salary has increased dramatically.

These are only a few of the hundreds of ways I have profited by my trained memory. No longer do I suffer the frustration of meeting people I know and not being able to recall their names. The moment I see someone I have met before a name leaps into my mind. Now I find it easy to recall everything I read. I can now master a subject in considerably less time than before. Price lists, reports, quotations, data of all kinds. I can recall in detail almost at will. I rarely make a mistake.

What Peter told me that eventful evening was this: 'Send for details of Dr Furst's Memory Course.' I did. That was my first step in learning to do all the remarkable things I have told you about. In fact, I was so impressed that I got permission to publish Dr Furst's Course myself.

My advice to you now is don't wait another minute. Full details of Dr Furst's remarkable Course are available free on request. Post the coupon today.

BOB HEAP

We, the publishers, have printed full details of Dr Furst's unique memory training method in a free book entitled 'Adventures in Memory'. For your free copy just post the coupon below (no stamp needed). Or write to: Memory and Concentration Studies, (Dept. IDM37), FREEPOST 246, London WC1A 1BR.

Free Book Coupon

To: Memory and Concentration Studies (Dept. IDM37), FREEPOST 246, London WC1A 1BR.

Please send me your free book 'Adventures in Memory', with proof that Dr Furst's method really works.

NAME

ADDRESS

POSTCODE

NO STAMP NEEDED

Text B

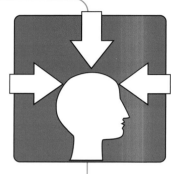

Do you realize how **easy** it is to improve your memory? Most people don't. In fact, most people do not realize the tremendous benefits an improved memory can have. They simply don't think about it; what they were born with is as good as it gets. Many people with poor memory usage may even think that they just aren't smart.

That's not true. **Anyone can improve their memory tremendously.**

If you noticed, we said 'poor memory usage' above and not 'poor memory'. That's because **everyone has the potential to have an incredible memory**. Most simply don't know the techniques that unleash this potential. By learning and using what we show you in our 'improved memory' document which will be available soon, you will be able to memorize lists of any number of items (10s, 100's, thousands); remember 10, 20, 50, 100+ digit numbers easily, learn how to never forget a person's name again, remember phone numbers, memorize entire decks of cards (suit and number) in order and out of order . . . Once you learn these techniques, the application possibilities are endless.

TRY THIS: Here's a quick example of a memory technique discussed in the document below:

STEP ONE: Think of an image that rhymes with each individual number from 1 to 10. Once you decide on an image, be sure to use only that image from then on. Here is the list that we use:

Ever try to remember 10 things you needed to pick up at the grocery store and when you got there only remembered a few of the items? That will never happen again if you use this memory method! It uses numbers, rhymes and imagery to associate the desired items and commit them to memory, for as long as you want.

1. NUN
2. SHOE
3. TREE
4. DOOR
5. HIVE (beehive)
6. STICKS
7. HEAVEN
8. GATE
9. WINE
10. HEN

Once you decide on your list, go through it a few times so that as soon as you say or think of a number, the image of the word you associated to that number comes to mind. You should be able to do this before going on to step 2.

STEP TWO: Now that you have a readily accessible numbered list in you head, simply associate each of your grocery items to the image in your numbered list. This is done by visualizing some sort of relationship between the two images.

For example, say you wanted to remember to buy the following: milk, coffee, bread, thumbtacks, light bulbs, oranges, gum, toothpaste, paper-plates and some flowers. This is how you might create the associations:

LIST IMAGE	GROCERY ITEM	VISUALIZE THIS
NUN	MILK	A nun drinking out of a HUGE gallon of milk, messily
SHOE	COFFEE	Drinking steaming-hot coffee out of a dirty old shoe
TREE	BREAD	Pieces of bread hanging from a tree instead of apples
DOOR	THUMBTACKS	A large wooden door which has thousands of thumbtacks stuck in it. Be careful opening it!
HIVE	LIGHT BULBS	Bees circling and entering a large light bulb hanging from the limb of a tree
STICKS	ORANGES	Kids playing hockey (sticks) with an orange instead of a puck (picture a real messy slapshot)
HEAVEN	GUM	A large stick of gum flying with angel wings
GATE	TOOTHPASTE	A huge iron gate absolutely covered in blue toothpaste
WINE	PAPER-PLATES	Knocking over a large glass of red wine which spills onto and seeps into your paper-plate, ruining your dinner
HEN	FLOWERS	Chasing a hen around the room that has a bouquet of flowers you just bought for someone in its mouth.

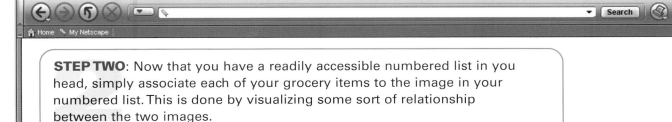

The point is to be as imaginative as possible for every link. ***Think creatively***.

STEP THREE: Once you have those associations created, all you have to do is think of the number (which will bring up the rhymed picture in your list) and you will see the silly association that you created!

What was number 1? (one - nun - gallon of milk)
What was number 2? (two - shoe - drinking hot coffee out of it)
What was number 3? (three - tree - slices of bread instead of apples)

You now know the entire list!!! And you know it in any order, too!!
What was 7? What was 5? 9? That's all there is to it! Congratulations!!!

If you have trouble recalling any image or association, be sure to go over this step by step again. Do not go to step 2 until you are confident about step 1, the same goes for step 3.

The example above is a demonstration of a basic memory technique, however it does not work well for more than 10 items (ie: 11 sounds like 7, 13-19 all rhyme...)

UNDERSTANDING THE TEXT

Text A

1 Who does the text seem to have been written by?

2 Who first made the writer aware of the possibility of improving his memory?

3 Name two ways that the memory improvements have helped the writer.

4 What do the publishers want readers to do next?

Text B

5 According to the text, who should be able to improve their memory?

6 Summarize the technique the writer uses to try to improve the reader's memory.

7 The technique described involves the reader in **visualizing** and in creating **associations**. Write down what you understand by these two terms as used here.

INTERPRETING THE TEXT

Text A

8 In small print at the top of the page it says *Advertisement*. Would you know without this heading that the text was an advertisement? Explain your answer.

9 **a** Why do you think the advertisement has been set out like a newspaper article?

   b Do you think the advertisement would be more effective if it was presented in a different way (e.g. using more images, less text, a different approach)?

10 What would make readers want to send off for the free book 'Adventures in Memory'? What might they hope to gain?

HINTS

- Think about what the book is supposed to do for the reader
- Focus on the ways it will help them in different situations
- Think about whether the reader has to pay for the book – what effect does this have?

Text B

11 This text aims to persuade us that we can improve our memory. Do you think it is trying to achieve anything else?

HINT

- Look at paragraph 3, beginning 'If you noticed', for a mention of something that will happen 'soon'

12 Text A tries to persuade us by telling a story about Bob Heap. How does text B try to persuade us?

13 Text B is taken from a website. Which of these possible audiences do you think it is aimed at?

- **a** people with poor memories
- **b** people interested in the topic
- **c** a general audience
- **d** a young audience
- **e** people who want to succeed in business.

Choose the one or two descriptions that best fit. Then write a sentence or two explaining your choice.

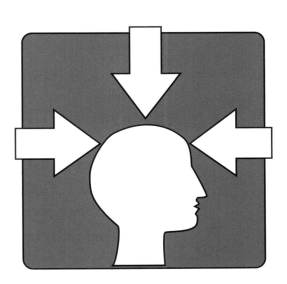

LANGUAGE AND STRUCTURE

Text A

1 Adverts are sometimes set out as newspaper stories. What features of layout make text A look like a real newspaper article? Are there any features that do not?

2 Persuasive texts often use the first person (*I*, *me*) to express opinions, and the second person (*you*) for direct appeals to the reader. Find an example in the text of each of the following:

 a first-person statements about the writer

 b second-person commands addressed to the reader.

3 **a** Find a sentence that is designed to inform the reader.

 b Find a sentence that is designed to persuade the reader.

4 Text A uses a story structure, and some events are related in chronological order like a recount. Find three examples of connectives or linking phrases that the writer uses to link one idea with another *within* paragraphs, and three examples where he uses connectives *between* paragraphs.

Text B

5 This text does not use a first-person story. Instead, like many persuasive texts, it addresses the reader with hints and suggestions. Find an example of a sentence in the second person.

6 Persuasive texts try to link their ideas logically to help the reader follow them. Find three connectives used by this writer to join ideas together.

7 Persuasive texts often begin by stating what they are about, and then go through key points in detail.

 a What is the opening statement of this text (look at the first two paragraphs)?

 b Find three key points which follow this.

8 The writer uses a number of sentence functions to give the text variety.

    a Why do you think it begins with a question?

    b From the first paragraph, write down an example of a statement.

    c From anywhere in the text, write down an example of a command.

9 The writer addresses the reader directly using an informal tone. Find *three* examples of words or phrases that show the writer is aiming the text at the reader in an informal style.

WRITING ACTIVITY

Imagine that Bob Heap, the writer of text A, has discovered the memory technique described in text B. He writes about it for a newspaper advertisement. Write the first two paragraphs of the advertisement.

Remember to follow his style:

◆ retell it as a story

◆ use the first person (I)

◆ use the past tense.

You might start like this:

Improve your memory — it's as simple as 1-2-3!

One evening after a busy day in the office, I was relaxing by surfing the Internet. I'd always worried about my poor memory, so . . .

Unit 5

Extended Writing

Imagine you have been asked to help promote a new interactive revision guide. RAPID REVISE is a CD-rom for every Key Stage 3 and GCSE subject, which:

- lets students identify their own strengths and weaknesses
- uses video clips and a talking examiner to guide users through essential knowledge
- uses fun tests and instant feedback
- allows users to build their own revision schedule
- costs £12.

It is being marketed in two ways:

- An article to appear in magazines aimed at young people.
- A website giving users a flavour of what RAPID REVISE is like.

Write one or both of these persuasive texts.

For the magazine article:

- Think of your target audience – young people aged 13-16. How will you grab their attention? What main image might you use? How will you use layout?
- Think about the language style – will you tell a story, or address the reader directly?
- Will you write in the past or present tense?
- How will you persuade readers that they must buy the product?

For the website:

- How will you present the information?
- What interactive features might you use?
- How would you make the site eye-catching?
- Will you use an informal or formal style?
- Will you address the reader directly?
- How will you persuade readers that they must buy the product?

Advice texts: the essentials

Purpose and audience

- Advice texts aim to give us helpful information.

- Texts may aim to change our attitudes or behaviour, or encourage us to buy a product.

- They may be addressed to a particular audience – e.g. a certain age group or gender – or to a specialist audience interested in their topic.

- Advice texts may share many of the features of instructions.

Text level features

- The text may use **illustrations** such as photographs and diagrams to help give clear advice.

- Often it will address the reader using the **second-person** form.

- To build the reader's confidence, it may use an **informal tone**.

Sentence level features

- To make the text more informal and more varied, the writer may use a **range of sentences**, especially simple and compound sentences.

- You would expect to find a range of **statements**, **questions** and **commands** in an advice text.

Word level features

- The writer will use some **description** where appropriate to make the advice easier to follow.

- Vocabulary will usually be **simple**, except where **technical terms** are necessary to discuss a specialist topic.

Health advice

A Sweet Tooth

OBJECTIVES

These texts offer different advice about eating sweets and your
health. You will be studying the following objectives:

- Word level: *unfamiliar words* (working out their meaning), and
  formality and word choice

- Sentence level: *variety of sentence structure, tense shifts,
  adapting text types*, and *degrees of formality*

- Reading: *bias and objectivity*, and *compare treatments of same
  theme*

- Writing: *anticipate reader reaction, present a case persuasively*,
  and *advice about options*

Introduction

These three texts all give advice about sugary food. Text A is from a
dentist's newsletter. Text B is an American website about chocolate.
Text C is an opinion column from the *Star* newspaper. They give
conflicting advice on what you should eat. When you have studied
them, you can write your own advice text.

Text A

A change in your diet could improve your next check up

The main cause of tooth decay is SUGAR. Every time you
eat or drink anything containing sugar your teeth are
under attack for up to one hour.

The frequency of sugar consumption, more than quantity,
is the important factor. It is best to limit sugary foods
and drinks to meal times.

Many processed foods have sugar in them. Always read the ingredients labels when food shopping. Sugar can be called sucrose, fructose, glucose, lactose, dextrose and the higher up it appears in the ingredients list the more sugar is in the product.

To limit the frequency of consumption of sugar in your diet and help fight tooth decay:

- If you do eat sweet things try to restrict them to meal times so the saliva produced can fight against the plaque acids.

- Try not to snack between meals. If you must, try raw vegetables, fruit, breadsticks, plain popcorn, low fat cheese or savoury sandwiches.

- Avoid sugary drinks between meals – drink water, milk, tea or coffee (without sugar: try one of the sweeteners if you can't do without).

- Also avoid strongly acidic drinks such as orange juice, all fizzy drinks (including diet and fizzy water) and sports drinks, which carry a risk of erosion of the enamel (dissolving the teeth). All these should be consumed in moderation. Never clean your teeth immediately after acidic drinks as it brushes the enamel away.

If you need further advice please ask the dentist or hygienist at your next appointment. Alternatively ask to see Becca who is studying to be a dental health educator - she will be able to identify causes of tooth decay in your diet and offer general advice on improving your oral health.

Text B

Three More Excuses to Eat Chocolate

You've always thought of chocolate as sinful. Now you can almost say it's healthy. *By Sue Gilbert*

Drink Chocolate Milk

1 Recent research at both Pennsylvania State University and the Southwestern University Medical Center in Dallas show that high levels of milk chocolate consumption do not raise blood cholesterol levels, even though chocolate is high in saturated fats. It seems that the predominant type of saturated fat in chocolate, stearic acid, does not have the same effect on cholesterol levels as other types of saturated fats.

Eat Chocolate Bars

2 Chocolate is loaded with antioxidant polyphenols. These are those same compounds found in red wine, fruits and vegetables that are touted for their heart-healthy and other disease-preventing qualities. Research presented at the American Chemical Society in March 1999 reported that chocolate contained, pound for pound, the highest levels of polyphenols of any food. In fact, a regular chocolate bar contained as much as an eight-ounce glass of red wine, or the same amount as five servings of fruits and vegetables. Cocoa contained the most, followed by dark chocolate and then milk chocolate. What is still not known is whether the polyphenols in chocolate can be absorbed by the body. Those studies are still preliminary and ongoing. Early results in animal studies are looking positive. This could be one science experiment where it may be fun to be the guinea pig.

Chocolate Is Better for Your Teeth

3 Chocolate is better for your teeth than other foods with a similar sugar content. Apparently the nature of chocolate makes it easily rinsed from the mouth by saliva, leaving it in contact with teeth for a shorter time. Chocolate also contains tannins, which inhibit the action of cavity causing bacteria, perhaps by not allowing them to stick to the teeth.

Text C

OPINION

It's sweets and sour . . .

SWEET-TOOTHED children are biting off more than they can chew – their teeth are rotting.

News from the British Dental Association that half of all five-year-olds and 90 per cent of 15-year-olds in the UK have tooth decay is alarming, but hardly surprising. Ask any parent who does not know the emotional blackmail which is created by a child bawling 'I want sweeties'.

Children become almost addicted to sugar with cravings for fizzy drinks and chocolate. Even if mum and dad are health conscious, the children still face peer pressure and resisting sweets displays at supermarket checkouts.

Dental health is important, which is why we owe it to our children to teach them about nutrition.

Stop before you buy them that next packet of sweets. After all, if you think they are crying hard at the refusal to give in, imagine the noise they'll make when they hear the dentist's drill . . .

UNDERSTANDING THE TEXT

Text A

1 How long do the damaging effects of sugar last?

2 Why should you try to eat sweet things only at meal times?

3 What should you do if you like the taste of sugar in tea or coffee?

Text B

4 Name two reasons the website gives that chocolate is 'almost' healthy.

5 Why is chocolate less damaging to your teeth than other sweets, according to the website?

Text C

6 What percentage of five-year-olds have tooth decay?

7 What two pieces of advice does the writer give to parents in the last two paragraphs?

INTERPRETING THE TEXT

8 All the texts are trying to advise the reader to do something. For each one write down what you think its purpose is, like this:

Text A is trying to advise us to . . .
Text B is trying to advise us to . . .
Text C is trying to advise us to . . .

9 a Which text do you feel contains the most factual information, as opposed to opinion or theories? How can you tell?

   b Which text seems most reliable and trustworthy? How can you tell?

10 Who do you think the three texts are aimed at? Use any of the descriptions below to help you define the target audience for each one:

mixed gender / single gender

young (below 16) / 16-35 / 35-60 / over 60 / no specific age group

educated readers / general audience / people with special interest in the subject /

people with something else in common

Give your response like this:

Text A seems to be aimed at . . .	because . . .
Text B seems to be aimed at . . .	because . . .
Text C seems to be aimed at . . .	because . . .

LANGUAGE AND STRUCTURE

1 Look at three headlines the texts use:

A: *A change in your diet could improve your next check up*

B: *Three more excuses to eat chocolate*

C: *It's sweets and sour*

The first headline addresses the reader directly.

The second offers a statement.

The third uses word play.

a Imagine text A using a headline with word play. Here is a terrible pun it could use: 'The tooth, the whole tooth and nothing but the tooth'. Why would such a style not be appropriate for this text?

b Why do you think the writer of B uses the adjective *more* in the headline? Try to explain what she is hinting at.

c Headline C uses word play. This creates a slightly jokey tone. Why do you think the writer does this?

2 Although advice texts are generally written in simple language, they can use technical/scientific terms.

a Write down three words from each of texts A and B which seem quite technical.

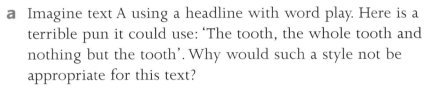

Text A	Text B

b How can you work out the meanings of these words? Can you understand them from their form or context, or do you need to look in a dictionary?

c What do you think is the effect of using these technical terms? Choose the answer from below which you most agree with and complete the statement:

◆ it makes the text more difficult to follow because …
◆ it gives the text greater authority because …
◆ it teaches the reader something new because …
◆ it makes the writer seem more knowledgeable because …

3 Most advice texts use the second-person form to address the reader. Text A does this:

Every time **you** *eat or drink anything containing sugar your teeth are under attack for up to one hour.*

a Why do you think the writer has chosen to use the second-person form?

b How might the sentence be written in the third person?

c What is the effect when it is changed into the third person?

4 Look at text B. Write down two connectives the writer uses to link one idea to the next.

5 Here are some of the language features of the three texts. For each one, try to find an example from the relevant text.

Sentence-level features

Feature	Example
a Text A uses commands, with verbs at the start of sentences	
b Text B also uses commands occasionally	
c Text A uses the present tense	
d Text B uses the present tense	
e Text C mostly uses the present tense. Find an example of the future tense being used.	

Word level features

Feature	Example
f Text A uses adjectives and adverbs to add description	
g Text B uses formal rather than informal words. Write down a formal word and then an informal word that means the same thing – e.g. Consumption (formal) ↔ eating (informal)	
h Write down some informal words used in text C, and try to think of formal words that might be used instead for each.	

WRITING ACTIVITY

Text B provides lots of information about why chocolate might be better for us than we thought. It is written in quite a technical style. Imagine you work for a chocolate manufacturer. How could you use the information to persuade people to start eating more chocolate? You might decide to produce a leaflet or poster encouraging customers to see the positive effects of eating chocolate.

Write one or two paragraphs for this poster or leaflet, using information from text B. Address your advice to people who like chocolate, but feel guilty about eating too much of it.

Use:

◆ the second person (You . . .)

◆ facts

◆ an informal style

◆ the present tense.

When you have written your paragraphs, re-read them and carefully consider the effect they will have on the reader. Do you need to change anything in your style or structure in order to make it more appealing to your audience?

UNIT 6

EXTENDED WRITING

Choose one of the topics below and write either a leaflet or a web page giving advice to the reader. Your advice should consist of:

a facts and statistics about the topic (you should research this)

b hints and advice on what to do.

Topics

Safe sunbathing:

* Why spending too much time in the sun is damaging
* How much time it is safe to spend in the sun
* Advice on ways of preventing burning

Exercise:

* Why exercise is important
* How much exercise people need
* Advice on different types of exercise

1 Choose your topic, then spend some time brainstorming ideas. To do this you could discuss the topic in a small group. If someone asked you for advice on the topic, what kind of response would you give?

2 Research the topic. It is important to give informed advice, which means providing factual information. You could use encyclopaedias; leaflets from supermarkets, gyms, or health centres; the library; the Internet.

3 Design your leaflet or website on one side of A4 paper. Make it visually interesting, but also clear and reassuring.

4 Think about how you will structure your advice: perhaps start with information, and then give your hints. Think about how you will use language. For example, will you:

* use the second person
* use a mix of statements, questions and commands
* use informal vocabulary which is easy to understand, rather than technical terms?

What are analytical texts?

Purpose and audience

Analytical texts give a response to other texts (e.g. books), to commercial products (e.g. a new type of car), or to media products (e.g. films). In schools, analytical texts are written by pupils to show their knowledge and understanding (e.g. history essays). Analytical writing often uses a broad question as its starting point – for example, 'What evidence is there that Lee Harvey Oswald did assassinate John F. Kennedy?'

Text level features

Analysis is often structured like this:

* opening statement
* exploration of the issue in general
* different key points discussed in turn
* a summary or conclusion.

When you are studying English, analysis of texts means exploring the themes, characters and language but not simply retelling the story. You will be expected to support points with evidence.

Sentence level features

The style is usually **impersonal**, using the **third person** for most of the analysis. The **first person** might be used for the conclusion. Texts are usually written in the **present tense**: 'Macbeth is desperate at this point in the play . . .'. **Connectives** will be used to help the reader compare and contrast ideas (*although, despite, similarly*) and to build arguments (*because, so, since, as a result*). They may also link to supporting evidence: *this shows that, we can see that.*

Word level features

Analytical texts will use relevant vocabulary for the subject under review – e.g. historical or scientific words, if appropriate. In English this will include **metalanguage** (language about language) such as *simile, rhythm, narrative*. There will also be vocabulary describing **judgements** – e.g. adjectives such as *entertaining, amusing.*

7 Analysing a process
How Rainforests Work

OBJECTIVES

This text analyses the issues surrounding rainforests. You will be studying the following objectives:

● Word level: *unfamiliar words* (working out their meaning), and *prepositions and connectives*

● Sentence level: *tense shifts*, *conditionals and modal verbs*, and *cohesion and coherence*

● Reading: *note-making formats*, and *trace developments* (of themes and ideas)

● Writing: *present a case persuasively*, *develop an argument*, *balanced analysis*, and *integrate evidence*

Introduction

This text on rainforest is taken from an American website called 'How Things Work' (http://www.howstuffworks.com), which gives information on complex scientific issues.

Look at the way the writer presents information about the topic, giving different viewpoints before reaching his conclusion. When you have read his analysis, you can write one of your own.

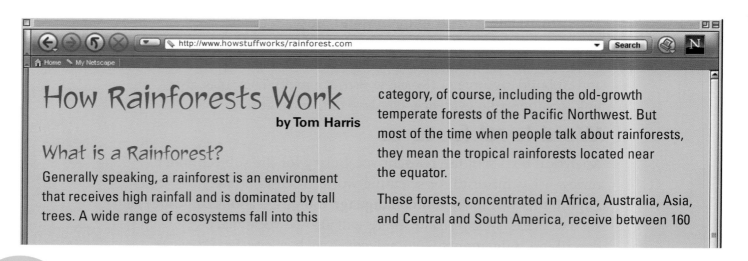

http://www.howstuffworks/rainforest.com   Search

Home   My Netscape

How Rainforests Work
by Tom Harris

What is a Rainforest?

Generally speaking, a rainforest is an environment that receives high rainfall and is dominated by tall trees. A wide range of ecosystems fall into this

category, of course, including the old-growth temperate forests of the Pacific Northwest. But most of the time when people talk about rainforests, they mean the tropical rainforests located near the equator.

These forests, concentrated in Africa, Australia, Asia, and Central and South America, receive between 160

and 400 inches (406.4 to 1016 cm) of rain per year. Unlike the rainforests farther to the north and south, tropical rainforests don't really have a 'dry season'. In fact, they don't have distinct seasons at all. The total annual rainfall is spread pretty evenly throughout the year, and the temperature rarely dips below 60 degrees Fahrenheit (16 degrees Celsius).

Deforestation

In the past hundred years, humans have begun destroying rainforests at an alarming rate. Today, roughly 1.5 acres of rainforest are destroyed every second. People are cutting down the rainforests in pursuit of three major resources:

- ❀ Land for crops
- ❀ Lumber for paper and other wood products
- ❀ Land for livestock pastures

In the current economy, people obviously have a need for all of these resources. But almost all experts agree that, over time, we will suffer much more from the destruction of the rainforests than we will benefit. There are several factors involved in this scientific assessment:

- ❀ To begin with, the land in rainforest regions is not particularly suited for crops and livestock. Once the forest is cleared, it is even less so – without any decomposing plant life, the soil is so infertile that it is nearly useless for growing anything.

Generally, when people clear-cut a forest, they can only use the land for a year or two before the nutrients from the original plants are depleted, leaving a huge, barren tract of land.

- ❀ Cutting large sections of rainforest may be a good source of lumber right now, but in the long run it actually diminishes the world's lumber supply. Experts say that we should preserve most of the rainforests and harvest them only on a small scale. This way, we maintain a self-replenishing supply of lumber for the future.

- ❀ Rainforests are often called the world's pharmacy, because their diverse plant and animal populations make up a vast collection of potential medicines (not to mention food sources). More than 25 percent of the medicines we use today come from plants originating in rainforests, and these plants make up only a tiny fraction of the total collection of rainforest species.

The world's rainforests are an extremely valuable natural resource, to be sure, but not for their lumber or their land. They are the main cradle of life on Earth, and they hold millions of unique life forms that we have yet to discover. Destroying the rainforests is comparable to destroying an unknown planet - we have no idea what we're losing. If deforestation continues at its current rate, the world's tropical rainforests will be wiped out within 40 years.

UNDERSTANDING THE TEXT

1 Look again at the first paragraph. The writer says that the word 'rainforest' has a general meaning and a specific one.

   a What is the general meaning?

   b What are people more specifically thinking of when they mention 'rainforests'?

2 How rapidly are the rainforests being destroyed today?

3 One reason that humans destroy rainforests is to create 'livestock pastures'. What does this mean?

INTERPRETING THE TEXT

4 The writer gives a variety of reasons why preserving rainforests is important. Re-read the text and make brief notes of the different reasons given.

LANGUAGE AND STRUCTURE

1 The writer uses two subheadings: 'What is a rainforest?' and 'Deforestation'. What purpose do these serve?

2 Like most analytical texts, this one is mostly written in the present tense. However, in paragraph 3 the writer uses the past tense.

   a Which connecting phrase tells us that he is talking about the past?

   b Which verb phrase is written in the past tense?

   c Which connective does he use in the next sentence to show that the text is moving back into the present?

3 In the last sentence the writer uses the future tense, starting with a conditional clause, like this:

   If deforestation continues . . ., rainforests will be wiped out.

   Why do you think the writer finishes his analysis with a statement expressed in this way?

4 Look at the word *deforestation*. Even if you didn't know what the word meant, you could make a good guess by looking at different parts of the word.

  a Write down what you understand *deforestation* to mean.

  b Using a table like the one below, write down what each **morpheme** (part) of the word means:

Morpheme (part of a word)	What it means here
de-	
forest	
-ation	

WRITING ACTIVITY

The writer has strong opinions of his own, and yet he writes without once using the pronouns *I* or *me*. What if he were writing his analysis in a more personal form – perhaps a letter to the government? How would his style be different?

Using Tom Harris's article as your source, write the first two paragraphs of a letter analysing the consequences of destroying rainforests, and expressing your opinions. Write it as a letter addressed to the Head of Environmental Issues. You might start like this:

Dear Sir/Madam

I want to express my strong concerns at what is being done to the world's rainforests. The evidence shows that . . .

Remember to:

◆ use the present tense
◆ use modal verbs to discuss possibilities: 'We *should* be working to . . .'
◆ use the first-person pronoun, I, to express your own feelings
◆ provide evidence, such as statistics, for what you say.

Giving facts and opinions

White Knuckle Rides

Introduction

This unit features two texts. Text A is an extract from a newspaper review about British theme parks. It appeared in the *Independent*. Text B is from the *Independent* website. It is a guide to the 50 best white-knuckle rides in the world.

The two texts have very different styles. Both express views, supported by facts and statistics. Compare the way they present the facts and opinions. When you have studied these texts, you can write an analysis to review them.

Text A

GLOSSARY

ascribed – *attributed*

contraption – *machine, invention*

cynical – *seeing the negative side of things*

The Complete Guide to British Theme Parks

Do you know your Hex from your Legend of Voodoo Mansion, Tidal Wave from Apocalypse? What's hot and what's not in Legoland and Gulliver's World? With so many sites to visit, it's hard to know where to start. Try here. By **Martin Symington**

WHAT EXACTLY IS A THEME PARK ?

A beast that defies precise definition. Loosely, we are talking about a sizeable area devoted to fairground-type rides, rollercoasters, amusements and live shows. At some, there is a common 'theme' throughout, such as the 32m plastic bricks that lend Legoland in Windsor its distinctiveness, or the stories of Arthurian Legend and the Age of Chivalry that underlie Camelot Theme Park in Lancashire.

At other parks, specific themes are ascribed, seemingly randomly, to particular rides. Chessington World of Adventures' 'Rameses Revenge', for example, draws inspiration from the enigmas of ancient Egypt in order to clamp otherwise sane people into a contraption that turns them upside down, hurls them in various directions simultaneously, then dunks them in a pond (on the other hand, perhaps the ride's title is a reference to the effect the ride has on a participant's bowels).

Blackpool Leisure Beach has been a bit cleverer, theming rides according to the whims of corporate sponsors. Hence the 'Pepsi Max Big One' rollercoaster, and 'Playstation – the Ride', where you'll need to leave your game console

behind if you want to be catapulted vertically at 80mph before experiencing a freefall descent.

The cynical would suggest that there is one common theme to every park: money. Theme parks are in the business of separating punters from their cash, not just through entrance fees, but by selling fast food, soft drinks, trashy souvenirs and digital photos of families screaming on rollercoasters. And, where money's concerned, the more crowded the park the better.

AREN'T YOU JUST BEING AN OLD GRUMP ?

Not really. At weekends, school holidays and other peak times, most theme parks might as well be called 'Queue Gardens'. Dedicated theme-park goers and rollercoaster fans may think nothing of waiting for up to an hour for a five-minute ride (some even claim that anticipation enhances the experience, in the same way that the smell of cooking whets the appetite), but children who have been anticipating a fun day out for weeks see things rather differently; they hate queuing. The best way round this is to avoid weekends and holidays if you possibly can. Wet days are also quieter.

Text B

> **GLOSSARY**
>
> **fraught** – *difficult, stressful*

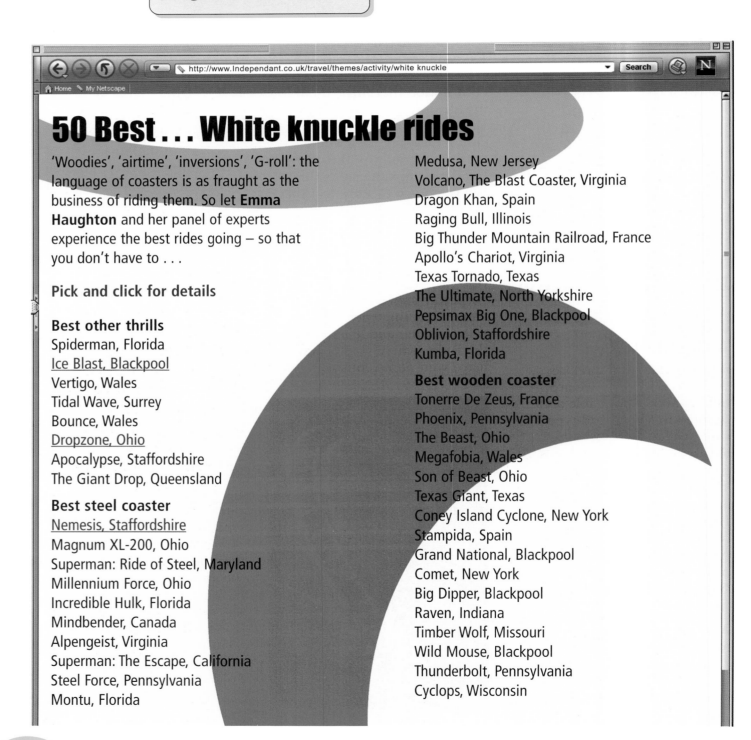

http://www.Independant.co.uk/travel/themes/activity/white knuckle   [Search]

Home   My Netscape

50 Best . . . White knuckle rides

'Woodies', 'airtime', 'inversions', 'G-roll': the language of coasters is as fraught as the business of riding them. So let **Emma Haughton** and her panel of experts experience the best rides going – so that you don't have to . . .

Pick and click for details

Best other thrills
Spiderman, Florida
Ice Blast, Blackpool
Vertigo, Wales
Tidal Wave, Surrey
Bounce, Wales
Dropzone, Ohio
Apocalypse, Staffordshire
The Giant Drop, Queensland

Best steel coaster
Nemesis, Staffordshire
Magnum XL-200, Ohio
Superman: Ride of Steel, Maryland
Millennium Force, Ohio
Incredible Hulk, Florida
Mindbender, Canada
Alpengeist, Virginia
Superman: The Escape, California
Steel Force, Pennsylvania
Montu, Florida

Medusa, New Jersey
Volcano, The Blast Coaster, Virginia
Dragon Khan, Spain
Raging Bull, Illinois
Big Thunder Mountain Railroad, France
Apollo's Chariot, Virginia
Texas Tornado, Texas
The Ultimate, North Yorkshire
Pepsimax Big One, Blackpool
Oblivion, Staffordshire
Kumba, Florida

Best wooden coaster
Tonerre De Zeus, France
Phoenix, Pennsylvania
The Beast, Ohio
Megafobia, Wales
Son of Beast, Ohio
Texas Giant, Texas
Coney Island Cyclone, New York
Stampida, Spain
Grand National, Blackpool
Comet, New York
Big Dipper, Blackpool
Raven, Indiana
Timber Wolf, Missouri
Wild Mouse, Blackpool
Thunderbolt, Pennsylvania
Cyclops, Wisconsin

Wild One, Maryland
Giant Dipper, California
Viper, Illinois
Riverside Cyclone, Massachusetts
Shivering Timbers, Michigan

The Panel
Steve O'Brien, 36, has been riding coasters since he was seven and is a regular contributor on **www.rollercoaster.com. Justin Garvanovic** is editor-in-chief of coaster magazine *First Drop* and founder of the European Coaster Club (**www.coasterclub.org**). **Andy Hine** is chairman and founder of the Roller Coaster Club of Great Britain (**www.rccgb.co.uk**). He has now sampled 90 per cent of the world's coasters. **Chris Cox**, 16, is a member of RCCGB and has experienced many of the world's best rides. He went on his first coaster at the age of six.

Best other thrills
Ice Blast, Blackpool
The UK's only 'vertical reality' air-powered experience, this £2m shot'n'drop tower stands at 210 feet, making it another major feature on the Blackpool skyline.
'More intense than Oakwood's The Bounce, this is a great way to be terrified and thrilled at the same time,' says Chris Cox. 'Definitely a must-have experience if you're ever in Blackpool.'

Where: Blackpool Pleasure Beach, Blackpool, Lancashire.
Ride duration: 1 minute.

Best other thrills
Dropzone, Ohio
Feel your heart plummet when you plunge 26 storeys from a height of 315 feet, straight down at speeds of over 61 mph. DropZone is the tallest gyro drop in the world – 'gyro' refers to the rotation on the way up, which gives you an outstanding view of the park and surrounding area. 'When it comes to freefalls, size does matter,' says Steve O'Brien. 'This offers the most gut-wrenching adrenalin-rush available.'

Where: Paramount's Kings Island, Kings Mills, Ohio, US.
Ride duration: 1 minute 28 seconds.

Best steel coaster
Nemesis, Staffordshire
Built in 1994, Nemesis opened as Europe's first suspended looping rollercoaster, and was voted the best steel coaster in Europe by the European Coaster Club last year. It cost £12m to build and runs for more than 2,350 feet, using 440 tons of steel. Riders are treated to an unnerving upside-down view of a blood-filled pool as they crest a 360-degree loop, which pulls four Gs on the way out. 'This is a classic,' says Justin Garvanovic, 'and it's so clever. The pacing is perfect and the terrain is used to excellent effect.'

Where: Alton Towers, Staffordshire.
Ride duration: 1 minute 30 seconds.

UNIT 7

UNDERSTANDING THE TEXT

Text A

1 Based on the article, is it possible easily to sum up what a theme park is?

2 What is the main difference between the rides at Blackpool Leisure Beach and Chessington World of Adventures?

3 How should visitors avoid queues?

Text B

4 Where is the Nemesis ride?

5 How long does the Ice Blast ride last?

INTERPRETING THE TEXT

6 Do the two texts give the same information, or are they really covering the topics differently? Finish these statements:

  a Text A is about . . .

  b Text B is about . . .

  c The audience for text A is probably . . .

  d The audience for text B is probably . . .

  e What the texts have in common is that they ...

  f They are different because they . . .

7 Analytical texts usually give both facts and opinions.

  a Find an example of a *fact* from text A.

  b Find an example of an *opinion* from text A.

  c Find an example of a *fact* from text B.

  d Find an example of an *opinion* from text B.

8 Text A is like a personal essay. Text B, for the most part, is much more factual. Which text do you prefer and why?

LANGUAGE AND STRUCTURE

1 Text A is organized in a question-and-answer format.

   a What do you notice about the style of the questions - how formal are they?

   b Why do you think the author has used this approach – how does it help him to communicate his message?

2 Text A uses some formal and complex words – such as *defies*, *devoted*, *distinctiveness*, which are all in the first paragraph.

   a Find three other complex words (words of more than two syllables, which are not very familiar).

   b What does this choice of vocabulary tell you about the target audience?

3 Look at the way text A is divided into paragraphs. For each paragraph, write down a few words to summarize what it is about.

4 The main page of text B is much more direct, using hypertext links so that readers can choose what they wish to read next.

   a Why do you think the writer gives so little text on the main page?

   b Write a sentence or two describing the way the writer of the website pages has organized the material, and how this is different from the way it would be printed in a newspaper or magazine.

5 How would you describe the way the reviewers in text B give their opinions?

   a their language is chatty

   b their language is informal

   c their language is quite formal

   d their language expresses their enthusiasm

   e their language gives an objective judgement.

Explain your choice.

6 Look at the box in text B reviewing Nemesis. The review combines facts and opinions.

    a For each sentence, decide whether it is a fact (F) or an opinion (O):

    1: 'Built in …'

    2: 'It cost …'

    3: 'Riders are …'

    4: 'This is …'

    5: 'The pacing …'

    b Why do you think the writer has organized the mix of facts and opinions in this order?

    c How do the speech marks in the review make it easy to spot the opinion?

    d Why do you think the writer includes 'Where' and 'Ride duration' as a separate paragraph of information, rather than building it into the analysis?

WRITING ACTIVITY

How useful do you find the theme park and rollercoaster reviews? What are the best features of each text? What important information do they give? What do they tell you that is unnecessary? What questions do they not answer?

Write a paragraph or two answering these questions and analysing the two texts, saying which you prefer and why. Give quotations to support your arguments.

EXTENDED WRITING

Choose one of the topics below and do some research on it:

◆ Students' opinions on the lunches served in your school canteen

◆ The television viewing patterns of people in your English class

◆ People's favourite type of chocolate bar.

This activity has four stages:

1 Plan your investigation

2 Do the research

3 Analyse the results

4 Write the analysis

You might work in pairs or small groups.

1 Choose your topic and plan your investigation. Decide exactly what you are aiming to find out. Set yourself a question – e.g. 'What do students think of food served in school?'

Think about how you will get facts and opinions. You might use interviews, questionnaires, school data, and other sources.

2 Do the research. Make sure you are using a fair sample of people, but not too many. Make sure you are gaining facts ('How much television did you watch last night?') as well as opinions ('What type of programme do you like best?').

3 Analyse the results. Gather the responses together on a grid or chart. What patterns do you notice? What surprises are there?

4 Write the analysis. Start by explaining what question you intend to answer. Keep the style impersonal. Present the facts and opinions, perhaps using graphs, charts and diagrams. Write a conclusion based on the data. Build comments and quotations into your conclusion to support your points.

◆ Write in the present tense

◆ Avoid using *I* and *me*

◆ Use connectives to link ideas (*also*, *however*, *despite this* ...)

◆ Use layout features to make your report as clear as possible.

Speaking and listening
Special assignment

> ### OBJECTIVES
>
> This special assignment gives you the chance to analyse something through a discussion. These are the objectives you will be studying:
>
> * Speaking: *develop recount*, and *questions to clarify or refine*
> * Listening: *listen for a specific purpose*
> * Group discussion: *hypothesis and speculation* (thinking about issues and ideas), and *varied roles in discussion*

Discussing qualities

In pairs, discuss the qualities of something that both of you are familiar with. Possible topics might include:

* Which is the best theme park you have been to?
* Which is the best soap opera on TV – *Coronation Street*, *EastEnders* or another?
* Which is the best film you've ever seen?
* Which is the best novel you've ever read?

One of you should describe the product, place or event, giving examples of what makes it good. The aim is to try to think about why something is successful. Don't just say 'because I like it'!

For example, if you are discussing a soap opera, comment on how it's made, the topical issues it raises, the quality of the scripts and acting, the editing structure, how tension is created and so on. In other words, present some **evidence** to support your judgement.

Your listener should ask you questions in order to learn more about:

a the subject you are describing

b your own judgement of it.

When you have finished your discussion, swap roles to discuss a different topic.

What are reviews?

Purpose and audience

Reviews allow us to analyse, comment, and show the strengths and weaknesses of something. This might be a play, a book we have read, or a process, such as a project. Reviews will usually contain analysis (an account of what we notice), plus a judgement (what we think of it).

Text level features

The title may ask a **question**: 'How does Shakespeare create suspense in this scene?' The structure will usually be a **logical argument**, considering one point at a time, backing up each point with **evidence** (e.g. a quotation), and concluding with a personal **opinion** or summary of points.

Sentence level features

The style will often be **impersonal**, using the **third person** and avoiding saying *I* and *me*. It will usually be written in the **present tense**. Reviews use **connectives** to organize points, such as *although, however, therefore, this shows that.*

Word level features

The writer will use technical terms – e.g. when discussing literature, words like *plot, metaphor,* and *personification* will be used. The writer will include vocabulary related to **comment** – for example, *I thought . . . I expected . . . I learnt that . . .*

Writing about literature

Macbeth

Introduction

In English you will often be asked to write about plays, poems and novels you have read. The idea is to demonstrate that you have understood the text, and to discuss your thoughts and ideas about it. A good essay will have an impersonal, slightly formal tone, rather than repeatedly using phrases such as *I think . . .* or *I like . . .*

The main part of an essay will explore different themes and ideas, supporting them with quotations from the text. The last section will aim to draw these ideas together. This section will probably be more personal.

This essay was written by Ben in Year 9. He was practising for his Key Stage 3 tests and the essay was written in timed conditions about Shakespeare's play *Macbeth*. When you have studied it, you can write a review of it.

Macbeth

In Act 4 Scene 1, Macbeth visits the witches to ask them to predict his future.

What do you learn about Macbeth's changing state of mind from the way he speaks and behaves in this scene?

You should think about:

- The way Macbeth speaks to the witches when he first appears;
- Macbeth's changing reactions to what the witches show him;
- What Macbeth's language tells you about his state of mind by the end of the scene.

From Macbeth's first reaction to the appearance of the witches, it is clear he doesn't like them. He seems to be horrified and yet fascinated by them. This is because witches were more real in Shakespeare's time than they are now. People today think of them as comic people with pointy hats and black cats. In the past they were much more threatening. Macbeth's fear shows this. He says:

> ' How now, you secret, black and midnight hags!
> What is't you do?'

He could have run away. Instead, he feels curious about who these 'weird sisters' might be. He also appears to be rude to them, addressing them as 'you secret, black and midnight hags'. This shows that he has no respect for them.

His attitude seems to change as they begin to make predictions. When they tell him to beware Macduff he becomes more interested. The witches may see that Macbeth looks shocked or nervous at this point because they say:

> 'Be bloody, bold, and resolute; laugh to scorn
> The power of man, for none of woman born
> Shall harm Macbeth.'

The witches are giving him advice on how to behave at this point. They seem to have a positive effect on Macbeth because he starts to believe that no one can harm him. He forgets their words of warning about Macduff. Macbeth didn't think this prophecy through properly, because he didn't think that Macduff could have been delivered through caesarean section.

The third apparition tells Macbeth:

'Be lion-mettled, proud, and take no care
Who chafes, who frets or where conspirers are.
Macbeth shall never vanquished be until
Great Birnam Wood to high Dunsinane Hill
Shall come against him.'

By this point, Macbeth seems to have become obsessed with himself and his future. He doesn't realise that an attacking army will cut down branches from Birnam Wood and use them to disguise their numbers. He has started to become arrogant, thinking that he is invincible.

When Macbeth finds out from the witches that Banquo's descendents will be kings, he becomes angry. He says:

'Horrible sight! Now I see 'tis true,
For the blood battered Banquo smiles upon me,
And points at them for his.'

Macbeth's language is full of fury. He uses alliteration 'blood battered Banquo' and this shows that he is aggressive, almost spitting out the words. By the end of the scene he is in a very angry state of mind. He has also become totally ruthless, shouting out orders to slaughter Macduff's family:

'The castle of Macduff I will surprise;
Seize upon Fife; give to th'edge o' th' sword
His wife, his babes and all unfortunate souls
That trace him in his line. No boasting like a fool;
This deed I'll do before this purpose cool.'

The scene shows Macbeth's changes of mood. He starts nervously, then becomes fascinated, then arrogant, and finally terrified. The witches leave him in a nervous state. After the show of eight kings Macbeth becomes extremely angry and takes out his anger on Macduff's family. It is not only his actions, but also his language which shows how power-crazed he has become. The actor playing Macbeth on stage would need to be able to show this range of feelings.

UNDERSTANDING THE TEXT

1 In his first paragraph Ben says that Macbeth feels two main reactions to the witches. What are they?

2 Why does Macbeth not run away from the witches, according to the essay?

3 What will happen with branches from Birnam Wood?

4 What point does Ben make about alliteration?

5 Write down a definition for a general reader of what alliteration means.

INTERPRETING THE TEXT

6 Good review writers should back up their arguments with evidence. How well do you think Ben supports his points? Does he use enough quotations? Are the quotations too long or too brief?

7 Literature students are often expected to say something about the context of a text – the period when it was written. Does Ben say anything about the play's context? Should he have said more, in your opinion?

8 When writing about plays, it is easy to treat them as if they are simply written texts rather than scripts to be performed. How well do you think Ben writes about the performance possibilities of the play?

9 What, overall, do you think the essay does well? How could Ben improve it? In your response you might refer to:

- structure
- use of quotations
- answering the question, and the way he develops his ideas
- knowledge of the text
- expression.

LANGUAGE AND STRUCTURE

1 Look at the first paragraph of Ben's essay. He uses sentences of different lengths:

From Macbeth's first reaction to the appearance of the witches, it is clear he doesn't like them.

Macbeth's fear shows this.

How does this sentence variety make his writing more interesting?

2 Essays are usually written in the present tense, as is most of Ben's.

    a In the first paragraph he also uses the past tense. Find where he does this and explain why.

    b In the last sentence of the essay, Ben uses a conditional verb:

        *The actor playing Macbeth on stage **would need to . . .***

        Explain why he does this.

3 The ideas in a review need to be linked and structured using connectives. For each of the connectives below from Ben's essay, write down what its purpose is. The first is done for you:

Connective	Purpose	
Instead (paragraph 2)	Shows something different – a contrast	
This shows (paragraph 2)		
By this point (paragraph 6)		
The scene shows (paragraph 9)		

4 The concluding sections of reviews often use vocabulary related to comment, such as 'I think'. Does Ben's conclusion do this? Do you think what he writes is effective?

WRITING ACTIVITY

Imagine you are Ben's English teacher. You have just read his essay. What mark would you give it? What comments would you make?

Write a detailed commentary that will help Ben to see how well he has done and also give him some guidance on what to do next time. Use the second person (*you*) to address Ben directly.

EXTENDED WRITING

Sometimes in English and other subjects you are asked to write essays. You will often be given a question to discuss, such as:

◆ *How does Henry V show his leadership skills in this scene?*

◆ *Some people think mobile telephones are an essential part of modern life. Other people see them as a menace. What are the arguments for and against them?*

This unit focuses on writing literature essays.

Your teacher will set you a specific title, based on a text you are studying. It might ask you to explore the way the main character changes, or how the writer builds tension in a particular scene.

Once you have your title, plan the structure of your essay:

1 Introduction describing the main issues or starting points (e.g. 'At the start of the scene, Henry is with his friends. He is part of the crowd, enjoying their jokes. He says: . . .'

2 Main body of the essay, showing how ideas develop. Each point will be supported by a quotation or specific example. Connectives will help the reader to see how one idea links to another (e.g. '*This shows* Henry's different behaviour. He is *now* behaving in a more distant way. *Therefore it is clear that* . . .')

3 Conclusion summarizing what you have learnt (e.g. 'As the scene develops, Henry's character changes. At the start he was . . .; by the end he is . . .')

Write your first paragraph. Remember to:

◆ use a topic sentence that shows you are answering the question
◆ use an impersonal style (avoid *I* and *me* until the conclusion)
◆ use the present tense
◆ refer to the context of the text where possible (e.g. details about when it was written)
◆ use connectives and linking phrases to structure your argument (*at this point, later, it is clear, however*)
◆ use quotations to support your points
◆ use a variety of sentence lengths to keep your style interesting.

How persuasive texts work

Persuasive language is used in letters, essays, advertisements, leaflets, television programmes, newspaper editorials and opinion pieces. Writers may aim to:

◆ express a point of view

◆ change your opinions

◆ get you to buy something

◆ persuade you to join an organization.

The text may use **illustrations** and different **layout features** to make an impact. The writing is often structured with an **opening statement**, and then **key points** will be described in more detail. The reader will be guided through the argument by **logical links**, and the writer may use **humour** to appeal to the reader.

Persuasive texts often use the **first person** to express opinions, but may use the **third person** to create a more impersonal effect. Advertising might be directly addressed to the reader by using the **second person** and **imperatives**. Persuasive writing will usually be **active**, use short sentences for effect, and be written in the **present tense**.

Writers will choose **emotive words** in an attempt to influence the reader, and **word play** may be a feature of advertisements.

Getting audience attention
RSPCA Radio Advertisement

OBJECTIVES

This text is the script for a radio advertisement that aims to capture listeners' attention and sympathy. These are the objectives you will be studying:

- Word level: *layers of meaning*

- Sentence level: *exploit conventions* (analysing conventions of text types)

- Reading: *readers and texts* (how they influence each other)

- Writing: *presentational devices, effective presentation of information*, and *influence audience*

- Speaking and listening: *compare points of view*

Introduction

Advertising is usually designed to entertain or inform us as well as to persuade. It is not always trying to sell us a product – sometimes advertising campaigns aim to change our opinions, or to teach us something new.

This text is a transcript of a sixty-second radio commercial made by an advertising agency for the RSPCA, a charity which aims to prevent cruelty to animals.

As you read, look at the way language is used to persuade listeners – and remember that the text was written to be heard on the radio, not read on the page. When you have studied it, you can write an advertisement of your own.

GLOSSARY

VO - *voice over*

MVO - *male voice over*

RSPCA Radio Advertisement

60 seconds

SWIM

VO: We are going swimming, my brother and I. We are going swimming with our best friend. But our best friend has not brought a towel. He has brought a sack. We are going to swim in the river even though it is very cold at this time of year. My brother and I run down the tow path. I can see my breath in front of my face. We are happy to be running as we don't get taken out as often as we used to. Our best friend seems to have less time these days. Now we are at the river. Suddenly my brother and I don't feel like swimming any more. It is cold. It is so cold that our best friend puts us in the sack to keep warm. I hope he does not slip because it would be very difficult to swim in this small sack.

MVO: Every year the RSPCA has to rescue thousands of unwanted animals.
If you give a damn, don't give a pet.

UNDERSTANDING THE TEXT

1 The speaker describes the way things have changed in his or her life. Name two of them.

2 Who are the speaker and brother?

3 Who is the best friend?

4 How can you tell that the weather must be very cold?

5 Explain in a sentence what is happening in the first section of the text.

INTERPRETING THE TEXT

6 At which point did you work out who the speaker was in the first part of the text?

7 What hints are there about what will happen eventually?

8 What hints are there that the speaker is very trusting of the best friend?

LANGUAGE AND STRUCTURE

1 The script is designed to be spoken. How far do you think the language feels like spoken language? Look at sentence structures and vocabulary.

2 How does the writer keep us uncertain at first about who the speaker and 'best friend' are?

3 The commercial tells a story using the present tense ('We are going swimming . . .'). This is fairly unusual for stories, which are more often told in the past tense ('We were going swimming . . .'). Why does the writer choose to tell the story using the present tense?

4 a How is the language of the last section ('MVO') different from that of the first speaker?

   b What is the function of this last section of the advertisement?

5 Advertisements often use a slogan to summarize their message.

   a How effective do you find the slogan: 'If you give a damn, don't give a pet'?

   b Who do you think the text is aimed at when it says 'you'? Is the audience general, or is there a specific age group or interest connecting the listeners?

6 This advertisement raises issues about pets and their owners.

In pairs, discuss the arguments for and against:

a owning pets

b giving pets as presents

Make notes of the different points of view expressed.

WRITING ACTIVITY

How would you present the message of this radio advertisement in a poster or magazine advertisement? What image would you use? What would your text say?

Draft a print version of an advertisement for the RSPCA. Use the same final slogan: 'If you give a damn, don't give a pet'. Decide on your layout, font style and sizes, and any devices such as bullet points that you will use to get your point across.

UNIT
9

Expressing strong views
Moving Target

> ### OBJECTIVES
>
> This article expresses a point of view very powerfully. You will be studying the following objectives:
>
> - Word level: *connectives for developing thought*
> - Sentence level: *punctuation for clarity and effect, paragraph organization*, and *exploit conventions* (analysing conventions of text types)
> - Reading: *note-making at speed*, and *author's standpoint*
> - Writing: '*infotainment*' (how information texts can be amusing and entertaining), *influence audience*, and *counter-argument*

Introduction

The writer of this text has strong views about car drivers and expresses them forcefully. Look at the way he constructs his argument and uses language to shape our opinions. When you have studied this opinion piece, you can write one of your own.

Moving Target
by Joe Gardiner

Roads aren't just built for cars. An irate cyclist pulls himself out of the gutter to remind car drivers of their selfish ways.

We wear the same kind of clothes, you and me; drink in the same bars, listen to the same kind of music. You could be my brother, mother, sister, or lover, but I hate you. While you are behind the wheel of your car you are everything I love to loathe – unobservant, inconsiderate, uncaring and above all, in the way. You see, I'm a cyclist.

Tell me, what do I have to do to get your attention? I've forked out £150 on a fluorescent jacket, I've got a halogen headlight, Scotchlight stickers on my crash helmet and enough flashing back lights that you'd mistake my seat-post for a school disco. But, like the plain girl or boy you're probably dating, nobody ever seems to notice me. Here's a tip – when you're opening your car door, look to see if there's anything coming, then look again to see if *I'm* coming. If you're looking for cars, you'll see cars. But you won't see a cyclist. So make like they did in the Seventies: 'Think once, think twice, think bike.'

As if this blinkered vision were not enough, I also have to contend with your selfishness. Not you? Well, see if this rings any bells – you're in a queue of traffic and there's someone waiting to turn right out of a left-hand side street – you're a considerate road-user so you wave them out. Tell me, do you ever look in your wing mirror to see if I'm coming up on the outside? No, I didn't think so. Remember, just because you're stuck in a jam doesn't mean that everyone is.

And aren't those cycle paths fantastic . . . for parking in? You might think so, but I've heard that doing so can result in your tyres deflating. I've no idea how it happens, but don't be too surprised if you leave your car parked in one and come back to find it with one or more flat tyre than you have spare.

Blind, self-centred . . . did I mention lacking in foresight? Here's a quick quiz – you're turning right at a T-junction, do you: (a) Stop behind the line, look both ways to ensure the road is clear then pull out; (b) Over-run the line by a couple of feet, stop, glance in each direction then turn; or (c) Roll out to the middle of the road while looking left, force the oncoming traffic to stop and make space for you, then pull away as fast as you can. From what I've seen, most of you think the correct answer is (c) although you'll occasionally be a little more considerate and go for option (b). If I had a quid for every time I had to swerve or stop to avoid being hit broadside by drivers pulling out of a junction I'd have binned my bike in favour of a personal helicopter. Once I've got up speed and gained momentum, I don't particularly relish having to slam on the brakes to avoid coming through your driver's side window. If I was a bus you wouldn't dream of pulling out.

That's not to say I don't enjoy the thrills of having to react with the speed of a cat to your clumsy steering. Mentally alert, I'm poised for reaction, the adrenaline racing through my veins as I tear up the miles. If I underestimate your gross stupidity and end up biting the kerb, I'll wear

my red badge with courage and pride and swap tales of pedal-power derring-do with my fellow cyclists.

A tale that crops up regularly is of you aggressively accelerating then swerving to overtake. This seems to be a favourite manoeuvre when you can see traffic blocking your way just ahead. Traffic should leave me free to sail effortlessly past, except that you seem to delight in positioning yourself on the road in such a way that I end

up stuck as well. Or, you just whip past, slam on the brakes and turn left, leaving me at a standstill in the gutter. That gesture you'll see me making means: 'Mmm. . . nice driving.'

Which reminds me – when I 'compliment' your road skills in this way then you probably deserve it. There really is no need for you to answer back or jump out of your car and try to batter me. Although the chances of you catching me on your pudgy, car-softened legs are small and the sight of you trying always gives me a laugh.

There you are, I don't like you and you probably don't like me either, but now that you know how much I 'enjoy' seeing you drive like an idiot, you know what to do. Improve your driving and show some consideration to me and other vulnerable road-users; motorcyclists, horse-riders and the like. Go on, you know it'll make me miserable having nothing to moan about.

UNDERSTANDING THE TEXT

1 What is the writer's main complaint about car drivers?

2 Who is he addressing in this article?

3 What steps has he taken to make sure he cycles safely?

4 Find an example where the writer uses sarcasm to make his point.

5 Find an example where the writer uses an angry tone.

INTERPRETING THE TEXT

6 Using a spider diagram, write down some of the complaints the writer makes about car drivers. Then circle the complaints which are most serious (e.g. pulling out of a junction in front of cyclists). Underline the complaints he has which are more minor (e.g. their legs are pudgy and small).

7 Do you find the article funny, or too aggressive, offensive, insulting, excessive ('over-the-top')? Write about your response to the writer's comments.

8 The writer makes a lot of criticisms, but does he suggest anything constructive? Apart from poking fun at drivers, what do you think his aim is?

9 What impression do you gain of the writer's character?

> ## HINTS
>
> - Look at what he says about himself
> - Look at the tone of the language he uses – what does this show about the way he feels?

LANGUAGE AND STRUCTURE

1 The writer uses an unusual style for his argument. He addresses himself to an imaginary reader and uses the second-person form: 'You could be my brother . . .'

What if the article was written in the third person, like this:
'Car drivers and I wear the same kind of clothes . . .'?

a Choose one paragraph and rewrite it using the third person.

b Say how the text feels different in the third person, and why you think the writer probably chose the second-person form.

2 Persuasive texts can use a very direct, informal style to get points across. This text sounds as if the writer is talking to us directly. Find an example of the way he uses language that sounds like spoken English.

3 The writer uses a wide range of punctuation, including quotation marks, ellipses (dots), dashes, and colons. Choose a sentence with one or more of these features and say how the punctuation helps the writer to express his ideas.

4 As with most persuasive texts, the writer builds his argument around a number of connectives and linking words. He uses informal phrases such as:

tell me   *as if*   *that's not to say*   *which reminds me*

a How do these links make his argument seem more personal and informal?

b The final paragraph begins: 'There you are . . .' Do you think this is an effective way to introduce the writer's summing up of his arguments?

WRITING ACTIVITY

Imagine you are a responsible car driver who has just read Joe Gardiner's article. You think it is very unfair. You think cyclists also often behave badly on the road. Write a reply to Joe Gardiner, expressing the driver's point of view.

As in his article, use the first person to express your opinions, and the second person to address your reader directly.

EXTENDED WRITING

Choose a topic that you feel strongly about. Some suggestions for topics are given below.

Your aim is to write an opinion piece like Joe Gardiner's, in which you have your say about a subject where you have strong opinions.

Possible topics

◆ Why attending school should be an optional form of education – people can learn just as well at home via TV, home study and the Internet.

◆ Why you should be given more freedom at school or at home – to behave like an adult you have to be treated like an adult, and given responsibility for taking your own decisions.

◆ Why people who smoke should be made to pay for their own medical treatment – so that there would be more money to spend on people with other illnesses.

When you have chosen your controversial topic, structure your main ideas into the order you will write about them. Think of the arguments you will use to persuade your readers.

Practise your style: Joe Gardiner addresses his readers directly, 'buttonholing' them with his ideas. Test your style in a few opening sentences, like this:

I'm sick of being treated like a child. I'm not a child. You tell me not to be childish. Then what do you do? Talk to me as if I've got a dummy in my mouth . . .

Surely there can't be many people on earth who don't know about the damage smoking is doing. You can't open a magazine without seeing a health warning. 'Cancer sticks, coffin nails' - isn't this what people who smoke call their cigarettes? Well, if you know how bad cigarettes are, isn't it your choice whether you smoke them?

Remember:

- The aim is to write something hard-hitting, lively, but not offensive – offending your audience will not persuade them of your point of view.

- You are not aiming to give a balanced view, but to get your own ideas across.

- Use the first- and second-person forms.

- Use emotive, dramatic vocabulary, and perhaps humour.

- Use commands, questions and statements for variety.

- Start with an opening statement and then move through key points, one per paragraph.

UNIT 9

Speaking and listening
Special assignment

> ### OBJECTIVES
> This special assignment gives you the chance to hold a debate about road use. You will be studying the following objectives:
>
> - Speaking: *standard English*
> - Listening: *compare points of view*, and *identify underlying issues*
> - Group discussion: (arriving at a) *considered viewpoint*

Debate on traffic

Based on Joe Gardiner's opinion piece, have a group debate on this motion:

It's time to get cars off Britain's roads.

Work in small groups to prepare opposing views for the debate. Different groups could represent different interest-groups:

- Car drivers (who enjoy the freedom of car travel)
- Cyclists (who want a safer, more environmentally friendly transport system)
- Walkers (who want less pollution, less noise, and less traffic)
- Rail companies (who want more business for trains)
- Coach companies (who fear they may lose business because of heavy traffic, unless cars are limited and coaches encouraged)
- Building contractors (who want to keep building roads).

Each group should put together the main points of their argument ready for the debate. Decide who is speaking about each point. Then hold your debate with each group having the chance to make its case, followed by questions.

Finally, try to come to an agreement about whether cars should be limited and, if so, to what extent.

How analytical texts work

Analytical texts aim to give a considered response to other texts, to products such as consumer goods and media broadcasts, or to events. In schools, analytical texts are often written in the form of essays.

Analysis is often structured like this:

opening statement

↓

discussion of the issue in general terms

↓

exploration of key points in turn

↓

summary or conclusion.

◆ The style is usually impersonal, using the **third person**. The **first person** might be used for giving personal opinions in the conclusion.

◆ Texts are usually written in the **present tense**.

◆ **Connectives** help the reader to compare and contrast ideas and to follow the logic of the arguments.

◆ Analytical texts will often use the **specialist vocabulary** of the subject under review – e.g. historical or scientific terms.

◆ Vocabulary describing **judgements** will also be used, with adjectives such as *involving, thought-provoking*.

Giving evidence and opinion
Road Transport

OBJECTIVES

This text is from the website of a pressure group, analysing some of the problems that are the subject of its campaigns. These are the objectives you will be studying:

- Word level: *ways of checking* (using dictionaries)
- Sentence level: *integrate speech*, *reference and quotation*, and *paragraph organization*
- Reading: *information retrieval*, and *evaluate information*
- Writing: *exploratory writing*, *explain connections*, *impartial guidance*, and *balanced analysis*

Introduction

In the previous unit we looked at a text complaining about the way motorists treat cyclists (see page 102). The text featured here also discusses the problems of road traffic, but in a different context. It comes from the website of Friends of the Earth, a pressure group which campaigns to improve the quality of the environment.

This document analyses the damage road transport is doing to the environment. It uses facts and statistics to support its case. It finishes with suggestions for what readers can do to help. When you have studied it, you can write an analytical text of your own.

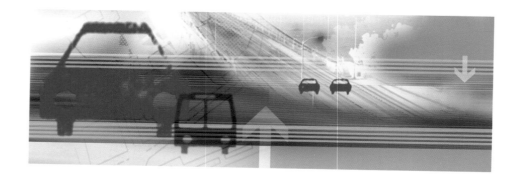

Road Transport, Air Pollution and Health

Introduction

Very few areas of the UK are safe from air pollution. Pollution levels exceed Government health standards all over the country on many days every year, even in rural areas. The impact of this pollution is huge: even the Government now accepts that between 12,000 and 24,000 people die prematurely every year as a result of air pollution.

Road transport's contribution to air pollution

Road transport is a major source of air pollution in the UK. The following chart shows the relative contribution of road transport and all other sources (other forms of transport, energy production, industry and domestic sources) to emissions of five key pollutants: particulates (fine dust and soot particles - PM), carbon monoxide (CO), nitrogen oxides (NOx), benzene and hydrocarbons (HCs)[1].

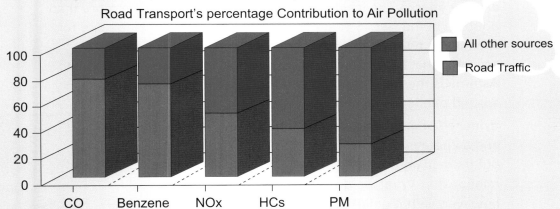

Road Transport's percentage Contribution to Air Pollution

But the chart does not tell the whole story. The contribution of road transport is higher still in towns and cities. In London, traffic is responsible for 99 per cent of carbon monoxide, 76 per cent of nitrogen oxides and 90 per cent of hydrocarbons [2].

Also when pollution levels are high, the contribution of road transport is often greater. For example, analysis by Government experts shows that when particulate levels exceed health standards, then road traffic's contribution is in the range of 75-85 per cent [3].

Road transport is also the main cause of ozone (summertime smog). Ozone does not come directly from vehicles or factories but is created by chemical reactions between nitrogen oxides and hydrocarbons.

Where is the problem worst?

Levels of nitrogen dioxide, carbon monoxide, hydrocarbons and particulates are highest in towns and cities, where there is more traffic. But this does not mean that rural areas do not have a problem. Levels of summertime smog are worst in rural areas. See the FOE briefing sheet "Summertime Smog" for more details.

Who is at risk?

The health of up to one in five people in the UK is particularly at risk from air pollution. These include young children, pregnant women, the elderly, and people suffering from heart and lung diseases.

Health impacts

In a recent report, Government experts concluded that between 12,000 and 24,000 people might die prematurely every year as a result of short-term exposure to air pollution. The report added that a further 14,000 to 24,000 hospital admissions and readmissions may also be caused by this air pollution [4].

One of the most well-known impacts of air pollution is an increase in asthma attacks. The incidence of asthma appears to have more than doubled in the last 15 years. Some of this increase may be due to changes in how doctors categorise asthma, but it is now widely accepted that the incidence of asthma has increased considerably. Asthma is the most common chronic disease of childhood with around one in seven children affected.

Evidence of a link between pollution and asthma is certainly accumulating, but there is no proof yet of a causal relationship. What we do know, however, is that pollution can aggravate asthma symptoms and can also trigger an asthma attack in people who are already asthmatic. There is evidence that use of asthma medication and hospital admissions diagnosed as asthma increase during severe pollution episodes.

Government health experts have concluded that 'there is a consistent, though modest, association between exposure to traffic and asthma prevalence in children' [5]. Other researchers have found that people living in streets with heavy traffic tended to suffer more illness than residents of streets with light traffic [6]. Similar studies in other countries have shown a relationship between the amount of traffic in an area and people with respiratory symptoms or wheeze [7].

How much does it all cost?

The impact of air pollution on health can also be assessed in monetary terms: the cost of health care, the cost of days of work lost, the economic cost of premature deaths. The National Asthma Campaign has estimated that asthma costs the UK over £1 billion per year [8]. Environmental economists have estimated the cost of air pollution from road transport at £19.7 billion per year [9].

What you can do

You can play your part in cutting air pollution from traffic:

- Cut your car use.
  Use alternatives such as public transport, cycling and walking;

- We are trying to encourage the Government to adopt policies which will deliver traffic reduction by encouraging MPs to sign Early Day Motions - on Company Car Tax, 'home zones' and CO2 emissions. PLEASE WRITE TO YOUR MP, asking them to sign these motions.

- Join Friends of the Earth and help us campaign for traffic reduction and cleaner cars.

Notes

return to text

1. Department of Transport: Transport Statistics Great Britain 1996

[Benzene figures from: Department of the Environment National Air Quality Strategy (1997)]

return to text

2. The Ashden Trust How Vehicle Pollution Affects Our Health (1994)

return to text

3. Quality of Urban Air Review Group Airborne Particulate Matter in the United Kingdom (1996) page 146

return to text

4. Committee on the Medical Effects of Air Pollutants Quantification of the Medical Effects of Air Pollution in the United Kingdom (1998)

return to text

5. Department of Health: Committee on Medical Aspects of Air Pollution Episodes Asthma and Outdoor Air Pollution (1995) paragraph 10.27

return to text

6. Whitelegg et al Traffic and Health report for Greenpeace Environmental Trust (1993)

return to text

7. Parliamentary Office of Science & Technology Breathing in our Cities (1994) paragraph 4.1.2

return to text

8. National Asthma Campaign National Asthma Audit 1996

return to text

9. Maddison, Pearce et al The True Costs of Road Transport

UNDERSTANDING THE TEXT

1 Like many analytical texts, this website uses some difficult and specialist words. Choose some words that are unfamiliar to you, look them up in a dictionary and write down the definitions.

2 Which statistic shows how serious air pollution is in terms of causing premature deaths?

3 Look at the graph on air pollution. Which form of air pollution does road transport produce *least* of?

4 What percentage of hydrocarbons is traffic in London responsible for producing?

5 What is the technical term for 'summertime smog'?

6 Apart from air pollution, what other explanation is there for the increase in asthma cases?

INTERPRETING THE TEXT

7 a Find five facts in the text about air pollution.

b How reliable does this text seem? What comments can you make about the sources of its facts?

8 Analytical texts often use a lot of facts and statistics to make their case. This text uses footnotes (small numbers in the text referring to notes at the end of the document) rather than including all the sources in the main text. Why do you think the writer has chosen to use footnotes in this way?

9 Who do you think the text is aimed at – general readers, people with a special interest in the topic, politicians, young people . . .? Write a sentence or two explaining who you think is the target audience.

LANGUAGE AND STRUCTURE

1 Look at the structure of the text:

introduction

analysis of the problem

↓

suggestions for what readers can do.

Why is this structure a good one for making the text seem reliable and informative?

2 Look at the first paragraph. How does the writer use language to show how serious the problem is?

> ## HINTS
>
> You might comment on:
> - the vocabulary the writer uses
> - the style of the first sentence.

3 Why does the writer use questions for some of the subheadings – e.g. 'Who is at risk?' Why are these subheadings a useful way of linking the paragraphs together?

4 In the paragraph on people at risk, the writer starts with a statement:

The health of up to one in five people in the UK is particularly at risk from air pollution.

Look at the next sentence:

These include young children, pregnant women, the elderly, and people suffering from heart and lung diseases.

Why does the writer choose these groups of people to illustrate the point? How does it help make the argument more persuasive?

5 The writer is careful not to express personal opinions, but sometimes quotes other people's views.

a Write down an example where the writer integrates a quotation of other people's views into the text.

b How does this help add authority to the writer's case?

WRITING ACTIVITY

The writer of this website analyses facts and statistics to build a case about road pollution. If you were writing a more personal opinion piece using the data, how would you express it?

Imagine you are writing a letter to a local newspaper about levels of pollution in your area. You are writing for a general audience. How will you use the information from the text and make your argument clear and powerful?

Write a two-paragraph letter, giving some facts from this text and your own opinion. You might start like this:

Dear Sir/Madam

I am writing to ask our local politicians to take road pollution more seriously …

End your letter by making recommendations as to what your readers could do to help.

EXTENDED WRITING

Write an analytical text which uses a strong base of evidence. Get hold of facts, statistics and other data to support your points, and try to convince your readers to agree with your conclusions.

You might choose one of the topics below:

1 Prison is not an effective punishment:

- ◆ Find data to show how many people are sent to prison.
- ◆ What alternative sentences could they have received?
- ◆ What are the re-offending rates of people in prison?
- ◆ What are the re-offending rates of people doing community service or under other supervision?
- ◆ What do you recommend should happen?

2 Alcohol abuse is a more serious problem than cigarettes:

- ◆ Find data about illnesses and deaths caused by alcohol and smoking.
- ◆ Look at the amount spent in hospitals treating both types of illness.
- ◆ Which creates the bigger problem?
- ◆ What would you recommend we do about it?

3 People should be encouraged to switch from cars to public transport:

- ◆ Find out how many cars there are in the UK.
- ◆ Research the amount of congestion there is.
- ◆ Investigate the costs of pollution.
- ◆ Suggest ways of getting more people to share car journeys or use trains.

Structure your essay like this:

Opening section

- Try to grab the reader's attention with a punchy opening statement.
- Set out what you believe the situation is.
- Try to make it impersonal (avoid saying I).

Developing the analysis

- Present the evidence. Use statistics, graphs, footnotes, and quotations.
- Use connectives to link ideas.
- Write in the present tense.

Conclusion

- Sum up the evidence you have presented.
- Make recommendations about what should happen.
- Address readers in the second person ('You could help by . . .') and suggest what they might do.

ADVICE TEXTS

How advice texts work

UNIT

11

Advice texts aim to give us information which helps us. They may aim to change our attitudes or behaviour, or encourage us to buy a product. They may be addressed to a particular audience, such as people of a certain age group or gender, or to a specialist audience. Advice texts may be similar to instruction texts.

An advice text may use:

- **illustrations** such as photographs and diagrams
- the **second-person** form to address the reader directly
- an **informal tone**
- a **range of sentence types** to make the text more varied, especially simple and compound sentences
- a range of **statements, questions** and **commands**
- some **description** to make the advice easier to follow
- vocabulary that is **simple** and straightforward, except where **technical terms** are needed for advice about a specialist topic.

Official advice

Sun Safety

OBJECTIVES

These texts give some government advice on health and safety. You will be studying the following objectives:

● Sentence level: *punctuation for clarity and effect, degrees of formality*, and *conventions of ICT texts*

● Reading: *evaluate information*, and *compare texts*

● Writing: *exploratory writing*, and *influence audience*

Introduction

Some advice texts have a deliberately informal tone – think of the advice columns in magazines and newspapers. But others give advice in a more impersonal way. They aim to create a sense of authority – reassuring readers that this is very solid, reliable advice.

These texts are taken from government documents. The first is from the Department of Health website, giving guidelines on avoiding too much direct sunlight. The second text is from a government website aimed at teachers. It is intended to help them teach students about important health issues.

Look at the way both texts present 'official' advice in an authoritative way. When you have studied them, you will be able to write an advice text of your own.

Text A

Sun Know How

✳ Home   ✳ Go back to referring page

ENJOY THE SUN SAFELY -
FOLLOW THE SUN SAFETY CODE

'Sun Know How' is an NHS campaign that aims to reduce your risk of skin cancer. Many doctors believe that four out of five cases of skin cancer can be prevented by following the five-point Sun Safety Code:

Take care not to burn

A tan may make you feel healthy, but it's a sign your skin is being damaged and it will lead to premature ageing of the skin. And you may find that you can't join in activities with friends because you're in too much pain from over-indulging in the sun!

Prolonged exposure to intense sunlight (or artificial UV radiation) can be bad for all skin colours - although people with black or brown skin have a lower risk of developing skin cancer - so take the following precautions:

✳ Shade your face to prevent heatstroke and eye damage

✳ Take care not to burn

✳ Shift to the shade around midday.

Are sunbeds safe?

The use of sunbeds is not encouraged as it could lead to skin damage from ultra violet (UV) radiation. You should never use a sunbed if you are under 16, have a lot of freckles or moles, burn easily, have a family history of skin cancer or are using medication that could make your skin more sensitive. Health and Safety Executive (HSE) guidance is that no one should have more than 20 sunbed sessions a year.

Cover up with loose, cool clothing, a hat and sunglasses

Seek shade during the hottest part of the day

Apply a high-factor sunscreen (SPF 15 or above) to any parts of your body exposed to the sun

What does SPF mean?

The SPF, or Sun Protection Factor, is a measure of how much a sunscreen protects your skin. The higher the SPF, the greater the protection. It is measured by timing how long skin covered with sunscreen takes to burn compared with unprotected skin. So, if your skin would burn in 10 minutes in the midday sun, using an SPF of two would double the time spent before burning to 20 minutes. However, you should use sunscreens to give yourself greater protection rather than to stay in the sun for longer.

Which SPF should I choose?

Choose an SPF with a factor of 15 or over. But limit the amount of time you spend in the sun, too. Don't forget to apply it thickly over all exposed areas and re-apply regularly, especially after swimming. Remember areas such as ears, neck, hands, feet and bald patch!

Text B

About   Search   HOME   Links   Feedback

Facts
Schools &
Curriculum
Links

Sun Safety

Introduction

The increasing incidence of skin cancer in Britain is an issue that affects parents and schools.

There are more than 50,000 new cases of skin cancer and 2000 deaths from skin cancer each year. Skin cancer is almost always caused by the sun. The increasing incidence of skin cancer in Britain is an issue that affects parents and schools. Prolonged over-exposure to the sun and episodes of sunburn under the age of 15 are major risk factors for skin cancer later in life. The British Association of Dermatology estimates that four out of five skin cancer deaths are preventable.

Sun awareness is a safety issue, and schools will want to prevent the possibility of sunburn while pupils are at school or on school trips. The best approach is one that combines:

- Education about sun safety. Learning should include knowledge about the sun, its effects on the environment and human life, the risk of skin cancer and ways to protect ourselves.

- Protection from the sun. Practical protection in the form of shade and appropriate clothing and high-factor sunscreen (SPF15+) is the most effective way of preventing sunburn and reducing the risk of skin cancer.

When discussing sun safety, remember that moderate exposure to summer sunshine is essential for our bodies to produce the required amount of vitamin D. This vitamin is very important in building and maintaining healthy bones.

Return to MAIN MENU

UNDERSTANDING THE TEXT

Text A

1 What is a suntan a sign of?

2 The text asks the question: 'Are sunbeds safe?' What is the answer?

3 What does HSE stand for?

4 Which SPF are you advised to choose?

Text B

5 What proportion of skin cancer deaths cannot be prevented?

6 What two roles should teachers perform, according to the text?

7 Why do our bodies need some exposure to the sun?

INTERPRETING THE TEXT

8 Advice texts are usually addressed to a particular audience. How can you tell that text B is aimed chiefly at teachers?

9 Both texts appear on official websites.

  a Which text feels more personal or friendly? Try to explain why.

  b Do both texts seem reliable as a source of facts? Explain why or why not.

10 a How do these websites differ from printed texts – what features do they have that you wouldn't include on paper?

  b Which one do you think makes better use of the possibilities of ICT (information and communication technology)? Explain your response.

LANGUAGE AND STRUCTURE

1 Like many advice texts, text A uses the second-person form.

   a Write down an example of a sentence from the text using the second person.

   b What effect does this have?

2 Text B uses the third person, rather than addressing readers directly as 'you'. What effect does this have?

3 Advice texts often use technical terms. Both of these texts use the term 'SPF'. Text A explains what SPF means but text B uses the term without explaining it. What does this tell you about the audience it is aimed at?

4 Look at these two sentences from text A:

And you may find that you can't join in activities with friends because you're in too much pain from over-indulging in the sun!

Remember areas such as ears, neck, hands, feet and bald patch!

Why does the writer use exclamation marks? What is the effect of using these?

5 Text B uses quite formal language in places. Look at this phrase:

Prolonged over-exposure to the sun

How might the same idea be expressed in a less formal way? Write down an informal version of the phrase.

6 Advice texts often use statements, questions and commands.

   a Find an example of each of these types of sentence in text A.

   b Does text B use all of these sentence functions?

WRITING ACTIVITY

Both texts use quite formal language. Imagine you were giving some hints to a friend after learning about the potential risks of sunbathing. How would you express your ideas in order to make your advice effective?

Imagine a conversation, and write down what you might say. Try to persuade your friend that he or she must be careful.

Then use arrows and labels to show which parts of your language are different from a formal, written, official text. You might start like this:

second person form – suggests a one-to-one conversation

informal opening phrase

You know, you've really got to be careful when you're spending much time in the sun. It's a lot more dangerous than it seems . . .

contracted verb form shows informality

EXTENDED WRITING

Your task is to create an authoritative website on an important issue. Aim to give readers useful and convincing advice.

You might choose one of these topics:

- How to revise effectively
- How to care for a certain type of pet
- How to maintain a mountain bike
- How to improve your diet and exercise patterns

Remember: the challenge is to create a website and, even though you will probably be working on paper, you need to think about the features and potential of ICT. You should include:

- ideas for graphics and animations that will make the message fun and more easy to follow
- layout features that are easy to navigate
- hypertext links so that readers can move between different screens to get the information they need
- interactive features – e.g. self-assessment quizzes and tests.

To be authoritative you need to use a fairly serious (but not stuffy) tone, and combine facts with advice.

Remember to:

- use the present tense
- use the second person to address the reader directly
- use the third person for impersonal effect where appropriate
- use statements, questions and commands
- use a variety of sentences
- keep paragraphs very short
- use a glossary to explain technical terms.

When you have written your text, review it with a partner. Decide what you have written well, and which passages could be improved. Which writing skills do you still need to develop?

How reviews work

The purpose of a review is to analyse something, comment on it and show its strengths and weaknesses. Reviews are often written of books, plays and films. They will usually contain **analysis** (an account of the features the reviewer notices), plus a **judgement** (what the reviewer thinks of its quality).

A review will usually be structured as a **logical argument**, discussing one point at a time, supporting each with **evidence** (such as a quotation). A review may conclude with the writer's personal **opinion** or a **summary** of the points made.

A review will often:

◆ use the **third person** for an impersonal style

◆ be written in the **present tense**

◆ use **connectives** to link points together in a logical way, such as *however, as a result, this means that*

◆ use **technical terms** related to the subject discussed

◆ include vocabulary related to **comment** when giving the writer's opinions.

Writing about texts
Not Waving But Drowning

OBJECTIVES

This unit contains a poem and a review of the poem, written in the form of an essay. You will be studying the following objectives:

- Word level: *terminology for analysis* (terms that are used for analysing language), and *connectives for developing thought*

- Sentence level: *complex sentences*, and *integrate speech, reference and quotation*

- Reading: *rhetorical devices*

- Writing: *impartial guidance, balanced analysis*, and *cite textual evidence*

Introduction

When you write about literature, the idea is to show your response to the text, not just say what it is about or what happens in it. This means balancing analysis (what you notice) with judgement (what you think of it).

Here is a poem to read, followed by a brief essay commenting upon it. Notice the way the writer of the essay makes judgements about the text and supports them with examples. When you have studied this review, you can write one of your own.

Not waving but drowning

Nobody heard him, the dead man,
But still he lay moaning:
I was much further out than you thought
And not waving but drowning.

Poor chap, he always loved larking
And now he's dead.
It must have been too cold for him his heart gave way,
They said.

Oh, no no no, it was too cold always
(Still the dead one lay moaning)
I was much too far out all my life
And not waving but drowning.

Stevie Smith

UNDERSTANDING THE TEXT

1 What has happened to the man in the first stanza?

2 What did people watching him think he was doing?

3 Look at the second stanza: what is the reaction of people to his death?

4 What do you think the man means in the final stanza when he says 'I was much too far out all my life / And not waving but drowning'?

Now read this response to the poem.

'Not Waving but Drowning'

The poem by Stevie Smith has a dramatic, unexpected title which immediately catches our attention. It makes us wonder what the poem will be about. The first line then helps us to make sense of the title. We realize it is about a 'dead man'.

The poem is confusing at first because it keeps changing point of view. The first two lines are written from the viewpoint of someone who sees the drowning man, perhaps from the shore. We are detached from him and the writer refers to the man as 'he'. Suddenly in the third line we

---

are surprised when the pronoun becomes 'I'. This signals that the viewpoint has altered. Suddenly it is the drowning man himself who is speaking, and he is explaining what is happening:

I was much further out than you thought

And not waving but drowning.

The dead man is addressing us directly, referring to us as 'you', as if we are the people on the beach who misunderstood his movements. There is something quite shocking about this – first, that the dead man is speaking to us, and second that the people on shore have let him die without realizing that he was in trouble.

The next section – stanza two – returns to the point of view of the spectators. This time they are looking back on their memories of the drowned man: 'it must have been too cold for him'. The writer uses understatement here – 'poor chap' – to suggest that the people on shore are not very upset. They describe the man's death in a very matter-of-fact way.

The last stanza returns to the viewpoint of the drowned man. It is like a reply to the spectators' words in the previous stanza. He explains that 'I was much too far out all my life'. I think by this the narrator means that he feels he was always out of his depth. He spent his life struggling to cope and asking for help. People always misunderstood him. They thought he was 'waving' when in fact he was 'drowning'.

The poem shows us how easy it can be to misunderstand people, to assume that their surface appearance is what they are like beneath. The poem also illustrates how difficult modern life can be, where everyone struggles to stay afloat, and few people really understand you. It is quite a disturbing poem, and more complex than the simple storyline at first appears.

INTERPRETING THE TEXT

5 The essay starts by commenting on the title. Why is this a good starting point?

6 The reviewer describes features of the poem – such as the shifting viewpoint – and also makes judgements about their effects, such as saying 'The poem is confusing at first'.

a write down an example of a statement or description

b write down an example of a judgement or evaluation.

7 Do you think the writer gets the balance right between describing what he or she notices and giving opinions – or would you have done it differently?

8 Review writers should use evidence to back up their arguments. How well do you think this writer uses quotations as evidence?

> **a** Are there enough of them in the essay? Are they too long or too short?
>
> **b** Are they used skilfully to explain the text to the reader?

9 The reviewer does not comment on the poem's rhyme scheme, or the structure of its stanzas. Write down one point the writer could have made about these.

LANGUAGE AND STRUCTURE

1 The structure of the essay is:

introduce the text

↓

analyse the text

↓

give a personal response

Write down three ways that the writer helps the reader to follow the line of the argument. Look for examples of connectives and linking phrases.

2 The writer uses evidence from the text in two ways: by using separate quotations, and by building quotations into sentences.

> **a** How does the writer set out the quotation to make it clear to the reader? Comment on the use of layout and punctuation.
>
> **b** Choose an example where the writer builds a quotation into a sentence, and describe how this works.

3 Although the review is analytical, the writing is quite personal. Sometimes the writer uses 'we' and later 'I'. How effective do you find this use of the first-person style? Would the essay be better if it seemed more impersonal?

4 Look at the writer's sentence style in the first paragraph of the essay:

> *The poem by Stevie Smith has a dramatic, unexpected title which immediately catches our attention.(1) It makes us wonder what the poem will be about.(2) The first line then helps us to make sense of the title.(3) We realize it is about a 'dead man'. (4)*

All of these are complex sentences, but sentences 2, 3 and 4 are all of similar length. Does this make the style seem a bit dull, and too much like a list of points? Try using a conjunction (e.g. *and*) to join sentences 3 and 4 together. Does this help to give variety?

Stevie Smith

WRITING ACTIVITY

What is your overall judgement of the essay? What do you like about it? What could be improved? Write a review of it, as if you were this student's teacher giving detailed feedback. You might comment upon:

- the structure of the essay
- the way the ideas are explained
- the use of quotations
- the vocabulary used
- the sentence structures
- the balance of description and review.

Try to give as much specific feedback as possible. Aim to balance positive comments with suggestions about areas that could be developed.

UNIT 12

EXTENDED WRITING

Read this poem by Frances Cornford. Then write a personal response to it, like the essay on pages 129–130. The questions below may help you to explore the poem.

A Recollection

My father's friend came once to tea.

He laughed and talked. He spoke to me.

But in another week they said

That friendly pink-faced man was dead.

'How sad . . .' they said, 'the best of men . . .'

So I said, too, 'How sad'; but then

Deep in my heart I thought, with pride,

'I know a person who has died'.

Frances Cornford

Frances Cornford

1 What do we learn about the character of the narrator?

2 Where and when do you think the poem is set?

3 How can we tell that the narrator is a child? How does the writer emphasize this?

4 Why does the narrator imitate the comments of the adults?

5 What is the poem telling us about childhood views of death?

Writing about the text

A Write an opening statement saying what the poem is about.

B Next, analyse the poem in sequence, following its development line by line. Aim to comment on the language used, what happens, what we learn about the setting, and what the narrator is like.

C Conclude by summing up what the poem shows us about the narrator, and what it shows about the way children view death.

- Use an analytical style, perhaps using *we* and I when necessary.
- Use both separate and embedded quotations to support your comments.
- Aim to use a variety of sentence lengths.

D When you have finished, discuss your work with a partner. Which parts of your review are most effective? Which skills do you need to develop further for writing about poetry?